A Concise Code of Jewish Law for Converts

קיצור שלחן ערוך לגרים

A CONCISE CODE OF JEWISH LAW FOR CONVERTS

Rabbi Michael J. Broyde

Urim Publications
Jerusalem • New York

A Concise Code of Jewish Law
for Converts
by Michael J. Broyde
Copyright © 2017 Michael J. Broyde
Typeset by Ariel Walden
Printed in Israel
First Edition
ISBN 978-965-524-249-2
Urim Publications, P.O. Box 52287,
Jerusalem 9152102 Israel
www.UrimPublications.com

Library of Congress Cataloging-in-Publication Data
Names: Broyde, Michael J., author.
Title: A concise code of Jewish law for converts / Rabbi Michael J. Broyde.
Description: First edition. | Jerusalem ; New York : Urim Publications,
  [2017] | Includes index.
Identifiers: LCCN 2016055439 | ISBN 9789655242492 (hardcover : alk.
  paper)
Subjects: LCSH: Jewish law. | Conversion—Judaism.
Classification: LCC BM520.3.B765 2017 | DDC 296.7/14—dc23 LC
  record available at https://lccn.loc.gov/2016055439

This work is dedicated to the many converts I have been privileged to work with over the past several decades.

Each and every one of them is a unique and special Jew and each of them contributes to the Jewish community.

The Tosafot (Yevamot 47b and Kiddushin 70b–71a s.v. Kashim) stress the special status of each and every convert with two very important observations, which motivate the writing of this work. First, acceptance of converts imposes a particular duty on born-Jews, since one who causes any anguish to a convert violates fundamental precepts of the Jewish tradition. Secondly, converts seem to be especially knowledgeable and scrupulous about mitzva performance. Their enthusiasm implicates those born-Jews who are less careful in their own observance.

Contents

אהבת הגר שבא ונכנס תחת כנפי השכינה שתי מצות עשה, אחת מפני
שהוא בכלל ריעים, ואחת מפני שהוא גר, והתורה אמרה "ואהבתם
את הגר" (דברים י,יט). צוה על אהבת הגר כמו שצוה על אהבת עצמו, שנאמר
"ואהבת את ה' א-להיך" (דברים ו,ה י"א,א) הקב"ה עצמו אוהב גרים, שנאמר
"ואוהב גר" (דברים י,יח).

– רמב"ם, משנה תורה, הלכות דעות ו,ד

Loving a convert who has come to rest under the wings of
the Almighty [fulfills] two positive commandments: one for
the convert who is [also] included among the "neighbors"
[whom we are commanded to love] and one because they
are a convert, and the Torah states: "and you shall love the
convert." God has commanded us concerning the love of
a convert just as He has commanded us concerning loving
Himself, as it states: "and you shall love God, your Lord."
God loves converts as the Torah notes "and He loves
converts."

– Maimonides, *Mishneh Torah, Hilkhot Deot* 6,4

Preface: The Halachic Importance of Loving the Convert

מצות אהבת הגרים: שנצטוינו לאהוב הגרים, כלומר שנזהר שלא לצער אותם
בשום דבר, אבל נעשה להם טובה ונגמול אותם חסד כפי הראוי והיכולת. והגרים
הם כל מי שנתחבר אלינו משאר האומות שהניח דתו ונכנס בדתנו, ועליהם נאמר
[דברים י', י"ט] ואהבתם את הגר כי גרים הייתם.   – ספר החינוך מצוה תלא

We are commanded to love the convert: In particular, we are directed
not to cause converts to suffer in any way, but rather to do them good
and charitably as they deserve and as we can. The converts are all
those who have joined us from other nations and abandoned their
religion and joined ours. About this group, the Torah [*Devarim* 10:19]
says, "Love the stranger [convert] since you were strangers."

– Sefer HaChinuch Mitzva 431

The mitzva of loving the convert is fundamental to this work. Most
sources that discuss this mitzva[1] indicate that it adds to the force of
the obligation to love any Jew – to love the convert specifically. The
question for a practical halachic work, however, is: "*How* should one
love the convert in particular?" Should one love the convert as in the
Midrashic parable of the stag joining the flock of sheep, recognizing
that the convert is always an outsider and will never exactly fit in?
Or should one love the convert as a long-lost member of a family,
who needs to be reunited with the community as if the convert were
always a family member, lest, out of loneliness, they return to their
original community?

This work adopts both of these alternatives as inherent to the
complexity of the mitzva of loving the convert – to love the convert
because a convert is different *and* to love the convert by helping them
fit in and not be different.

The first way of loving calls for heightening the pace and the

---

1. See for example: Rambam (Aseh 207) and the Sefer HaChinuch (431).

degree of integration of the convert within the Jewish community, so that they are no longer perceived as a convert. This complements one of the basic purposes of the mitzva to love the convert: to make sure that the convert remains part of the Jewish community and does not feel out of place or like a stranger. This is the basic message of Rambam's famous letter to Rabbi Ovadia (the Convert) directing him to pray in a similar manner as all other Jews.[2] Thus, in all situations in which there is a dispute about the mandates of Jewish law, this work follows this halachic factor in preferring to adopt the normative Jewish law view which brings the convert to further integration into the Jewish people. The view that highlights the convert's status as an outsider is generally disfavored, while that which encourages integration is generally favored. As Rabbi Feinstein (cited below in the introduction) taught: The mitzva to love the convert obligates us to resolve disputed Jewish laws (where a convert is involved) in a way that further helps the convert find their place within the community.

However, in certain situations, the convert's status as a stranger within our community creates an affirmative need of assistance navigating law, custom, and nuance. Ignoring that fact in the name of purely formalist equal status – pretending that the convert is not a convert – is not truly loving. For example, Shulchan Aruch (OC 529) records that when the Jewish festivals (*chagim*) arrive, there is a particular duty to reach out to invite the convert into one's home for festival meals. When all others are celebrating with family, one must manifest the love of the convert in particular by acknowledging that they need special attention. To ignore a person's status as a convert when everybody else is family-focused does not manifest love and integration of the convert as an insider; it simply causes the convert to focus on his family-less status. This work recognizes this reality and takes into account that the duty to love the convert sometimes requires highlighting the fact that this person is a convert.[3]

This is the two-sided nature of the duty to love the convert: One must both welcome the convert as an outsider, as well as do one's best to help them cease being an outsider. This work is aware of both ways of fulfilling the obligation to love the convert and factors them both into its determinations of normative Jewish law.

---

2. This letter is discussed at length in the supplemental essay on the proper Jewish-identity blessing for a convert.

3. The Sefer Hachinuch (431) notes that the model for how we treat the convert is a measure of how we always treat the stranger who is different (who may include *ba'alei teshuva*, new neighbors in a community, travelers, guests, and *olim* to Israel). We all bear a duty to be kind to the strangers around us.

A Roadmap to this Book

This work is arranged as follows:

1. Opens with an introduction that presents:
   - a structure composed of six undergirding questions, through which all this information has been collected and organized;
   - a filter composed of four undergirding principles regarding converts, through which all the issues have been analyzed; and
   - two practical keys that have served to deciding the law normatively.

2. Follows with the main section – a Law Code that discusses the halachic issues in which a convert may have a different standing than a born-Jew, or may have a different effect upon a situation than a born-Jew.
   - The main body of this code follows the order of the four divisions of the Shulchan Aruch Code of Jewish Law as outlined in its table of contents.
   - It is followed by four appendices of rule lists:
     A a checklist of the transition rules that a convert encounters;
     B laws related to the Temple or Messianic times;
     C rules for the son or daughter carried as a pregnant woman converted;
     D assets of a convert who dies with no Jewish heirs (*nichsei hager*).

3. The third section presents supplemental essays that help explain the Jewish law discourse on some of the issues raised in the Law Code sections. Even as the material in the Law Code is written for any reader who ponders matters of Jewish law, and can be

understood independently of the supplemental essays, these more complex and detailed essays provide further background for those who wish to study these and related issues more deeply:

- The first essay (co-authored with Rabbi Dr. Mark Goldfeder) focuses on the issues related to the text of prayer that a convert should recite.
- The second essay discusses the types of rabbinical court on which a convert may serve.
- The third essay discusses the status of a child born to two converts who marry.
- The final essay discusses whether the daughter of a Jewish woman and a Gentile man may marry a Kohen.

ONE IMPORTANT LINGUISTIC NOTE:

Throughout this work, the term "convert" is used to denote either a male or a female, but the Hebrew terms *ger* (male convert) and *giyoret* (female convert) is used when the rule discussed applies to only one gender.

WORKS REGULARLY CITED AND ABBREVIATIONS

The following works are regularly cited in this work:

(1) Rabbi Naftali Hofner, *Dinai Hagiyur vehaGer* (Tel Aviv, 5760) (DHG)

(2) Rabbi Yair Leor Ovadia, *Sefer Gerai HaTzedek* (Holen, 5772) (SGTz)

(3) Rabbi Michael Peretz, *Otzar Piskai Gerim* (Mexico City, 5768) (OPG)

(4) Rabbi Shmuel Eliezer Stern, *Sefer Gerut Kehalacha* (Benai Brak, 5758) (SGK)

(5) Rabbi Yoel Schwartz, *Madrich LeGer* (Jerusalem, 5770) (MLG)

(6) Rabbi Avigal Zecharya, *Gerut VeGerim* (Jerusalem, 5768) (GvG)

(7) Rabbi Moshe Klein, *Mishnat HaGer* (Jerusalem, 5769) (MhG)

(8) Rabbi Yitzchak Yosef, *Klalai Hagiyuir* (Kenes Hadayanim, 5775 (5775) (KhG).

All Talmudic references are to the Bavli unless the contrary is noted, and the Shulchan Aruch is frequently abbreviated in the notes as SA, with the various sections abbreviated as follows: Orach Chaim (OC), Yoreh Deah (YD), Even Ha'ezer (EH), and Choshen Mishpat (CM).

Introduction

Modern Jewish life in America has a number of unique characteristics, almost unprecedented historically. One of those unique features is the social ease with which one can convert to Judaism. People can and do change religions without almost any social, economic, or political complications. Indeed, studies show that people in America change their faiths frequently, and conversion to Judaism is no exception. This is a new historical reality of American Jewish life, and is still quite different from the reality in other parts of the world.

The present work addresses this new reality by filling a lacuna in the halachic literature[1] both for converts and for fellow Jews relating to converts. It collects the many different halachic issues that relate to the status of converts *after their conversion*. It discusses all the cases in which the halachic rules are different (or even where some authorities are of the opinion that the halachic rules are different) for a convert than they are for a born-Jew, or for how a born-Jew is to relate to a convert rather than to a born-Jew. It offers normative rulings that are applicable today for all of these questions.

The present work has: (a) collected all this information by asking six undergirding questions, (b) discussed all issues through the prism of four filtering principles regarding converts, and (c) offered normative rulings on the basis of two key factors to decide the law.

Six Undergirding Questions

The halachic issues in which the rules for a convert or for other Jews relating to converts are not the same as for, or toward, a born-Jew can be divided into six questions:

---

1. See page 173, "A Short Note on the Intellectual History of This Work" for more on this.

1. THE CONVERT'S RELATIONSHIP WITH THE FAMILY OF ORIGIN

There are certain mitzvot that are applied *in toto* differently to a convert, since the family of origin is not Jewish. For example: How should one respect and honor their Gentile parents? Must a convert mourn for their parents in the same way that a born-Jew does? Such questions[2] apply no matter how recently a person converted and no matter how well-integrated they are within the Jewish community.

The basic question here is how to approach the unusual family situation of a convert.

2. THE UNIQUE OBLIGATION TO LOVE A CONVERT

There are mitzvot incumbent on born-Jews in their relationships with converts. The most striking is the special obligation to love a convert. The duty to love the convert is complex in that love sometimes calls for singling out a convert for special attention, and not doing so at other times, depending on how the convert will respond to that unique attention.

The core question here is when to identify or single out a convert as such, and when to avoid doing so.[3]

---

2. See for examples: OC 116 (prayer for Gentile parents), OC 135 (status of converted child of a Kohen or Levi father), OC 141 (calling two biological brothers in succession up to the Torah reading), OC 432 (application of the fast of firstborns), YD 146 (inheriting pagan objects), YD 240 (honoring one's Gentile parents), YD 240 (honoring one's Jewish father), YD 251 (charity to one's Gentile relatives), YD 305 (status of first child born after conversion), YD 374 (mourning and kaddish for biological relatives), EH 4 (relevance of an Egyptian background of a convert), EH 22 (being alone with biological relatives of the opposite gender), EH 129 (identifying parents in a divorce *get* or wedding *ketubah*), CM 277 (inheritance), CM 282 (inheritance), CM 283 (inheritance).

3. See for example: OC 39 (status of a convert who returns to his old faith), OC 139 (how to call a convert up to the Torah reading), OC 529 (obligation to care for the convert before festivals), YD 1 (status of a convert who apostatizes), YD 171 (convert's obligation to pay interest to which he indebted himself as a Gentile), YD 217 (status as a descendant of Abraham as regards vows), YD 240 (marrying a convert), YD 244 (standing out of respect for a convert), YD 251 (priority for receiving charity), YD 268 (status of a convert who abandons Judaism), YD 268 (injunction against taunting a convert about his pre-conversion conduct), YD 268 (convert sitting on a rabbinical court for conversion), CM 28

3. TRANSITION ISSUES IN BEING A JEW WHO HAD BEEN A GENTILE

There are some transitional questions present in conversions, reflecting the fact that a person who was previously a Gentile becomes, in a single moment, Jewish and obligated in Jewish Law. For example: May a convert eat the kosher food they cooked the morning before the conversion, or is it prohibited to the convert as a form of *bishul akum* (food cooked by a Gentile)? What are the prayer and blessing obligations of someone who converts in the middle of the time specified for performance of time-bound mitzvot, such as in the middle of the day, in the middle of *sefira*, in the middle of Chanuka, and so on?[4]

The complicated question here is how to handle the situation in which a convert joins Judaism in the middle of an ongoing mitzva, or in which they must relate to their past self. (Fortunately, although these issues are beguiling, they are also transitory.)

(credibility of convert), CM 228 (sin of tormenting a convert), CM 97 (pestering a convert to repay loans). Logic would indicate that a convert is also obligated in the mitzva to love the convert, although there is no clear source to that effect.

4. See for example: OC 25 (prayer after conversion if one had already prayed), OC 47 (Torah blessings after conversion if one had already blessed these before conversion), OC 60 (repeating nighttime *Shema* after conversion), OC 199 (blessing Grace after Meals after conversion if one had eaten shortly beforehand), OC 232 (eating before praying the afternoon *mincha* after conversion even if one had already prayed that morning), OC 294 (ending Shabbat verbally [*Havdalah*] after conversion if one had not been Jewish on Shabbat), OC 370 (Eruv), OC 417 (Rosh Chodesh conversion), OC 431 (conversion on Erev Pesach), OC 489 (counting the *omer*), OC 495 (converting on *chol hamoed*), OC 496 (a person who lives outside Israel converting in Israel before Yom Tov), OC 566 (whether one who converts in the course of a fast day must fast), OC 612 (whether one who converts on Yom Kippur must fast a mere part of the day [even if they have been fasting since the beginning]), OC 637 (converting on Sukkot), OC 671 (converting on Chanuka), OC 687 (Purim day conversion), YD 61 (priestly gifts), YD 113 (status of food cooked before conversion), YD 120 (whether one who converts must also immerse their dishes), YD 121 (*kashering* dishes), YD 123 (status of wine opened before conversion), YD 171 (converting as a creditor or debtor), YD 183 (*nidda*), YD 189 (*veset*), YD 217 (obligation to fulfill vows made before conversion), YD 318 (firstborn animals born before owner's conversion), CM 259 (returning lost property that was found before conversion).

4. MARRIAGE LAWS FOR A CONVERT

There are certain people whom a convert may marry that a born-Jew
may not marry, and there are certain people whom a convert may not
marry that a born-Jew may marry. For example: a convert may marry
a *mamzer*, and a female convert may not marry a Kohen.

The core question is whom Jews who are converts may marry, since
converts are not Kohanim, Levites, or Israelites.

5. LIMITATIONS ON CONVERTS HOLDING POSITIONS OF AUTHORITY

Many societies exclude those members who were not born into the
society from holding some powerful offices. (One such society is that
of the United States.[5]) In parallel: the Torah tells us that a convert
may not become a king of the Jewish nation, and the Talmud rules
that a convert may not serve in any position of binding coercive authority. For example: a convert may not serve on certain kinds of
rabbinical courts. See CM 7 and 8.

The core question is one of contemporary Jewish law: what are the
modern day offices (or officers, or holders of certain titles) that fit
into this Talmudic rule?

6. A CONVERT AND PRAYERS THAT SPEAK OF ANCESTRAL JUDAISM

There is an ongoing dispute as to whether and when a convert recites
specific parts of the traditional prayers that reference Jewish ancestors or born Jewishness. For example: Does a convert bless God for
having been made a Jew (*shelo asani goy*)?

The core questions are when and why a convert is called upon to
identify themself in prayer as a descendant of the earliest forefathers
of the Jews, or as a descendent of the slaves redeemed from Egypt,
and when and why to identify themself as an outsider by birth.

---

5. For example, in the United States, only natural born citizens can be President
(section 1 of article two of the United States Constitution states: "No person
except a natural born Citizen, or a Citizen of the United States . . . shall be eligible
to the Office of President") or Vice President (The Twelfth Amendment states:
"No person constitutionally ineligible to the office of President shall be eligible
to that of Vice-President of the United States").

Four Undergirding Principles
Regarding Converts

There are four principles through which these questions are filtered:

1. Love: **There is a special obligation to love the convert,**[6] and there is a special obligation not to allow a convert to suffer because they converted. There are many explanations for this mitzva. The two primary ones are love of the convert and fear that the convert might abandon their Judaism for their original faith.

The following midrash offers a parable to explain the obligation to love the convert as a form of endearment:[7]

> A king has many flocks of sheep, and one day a stag appears and joins the sheep. The stag grazes with the sheep and returns with them at night, as if he were a sheep. When the shepherds tell the king of the

---

6. See Rambam, Sefer Hamitzvot 307. For more on this obligation, see Rabbi Gedalia Dov Schwartz's excellent work, אהבת הגר; Loving the Convert: Converts to Judaism and Our Relationship to Them, distributed by the Chicago Rabbinical Council.

There is also a view that the mitzva to love a convert applies whenever someone wants to convert, even if they have not yet converted (see Rabbi Yitzchak Albartzuloni as cited in Rabbi Yerucham Perlow's commentary on *Sefer Hamitzvot* of Rav Saadya Gaon, mitzva 19). However, that view is contradicted by the consensus grounded in the formulation of the Rambam (Deot 4:4), which limits this mitzva to a person who is now Jewish (for example, see Mishna Berura 156:4). In any case, this dispute, while generally of great importance, is of little importance to this work, since a person before conversion is certainly not governed by Jewish law and is thus excluded from almost all of the topics discussed here.

Having said that, it is clear that on a religious-ethical level that even Rambam would agree that it is proper to treat a person who is seeking to convert with the utmost love, sensitivity, kindness and *chesed*, as they are like a stag who is considering leaving their flock (see the midrash cited below).

It is worth adding that there is a contrary view in the *Rishonim* that denies that there is a mitzva to love a convert uniquely. This view argues that the primary duty is to treat the convert absolutely identically to a born-Jew, with no favoritism in any direction. See Commentary of R. Yerucham Perlow on Rabbi Saadya Gaon's *Book of Commandments, Aseh* 82. Normative Jewish law rejects this view based on Rambam's and others' incorporation of the special duty to love the convert into Jewish law.

7. Bamidbar Rabba 8:2.

stag, the king takes great pride and interest in it and ensures that the
shepherds treat the stag with special care. The shepherds question the
king, asking "you have thousands of animals over which you take no
personal interest, so why do you care so much about this one animal?"
The king answers them, "My sheep have only this flock to join, and
cannot leave, but this stag has the whole world to choose from, yet
he chose my flock. He surely deserves my special attention and care."

The midrash concludes that we, as the Jewish people, should give
tremendous credit to the convert who has chosen to leave their family
and their people to join our ranks. This is why the convert deserves
special consideration and care.

Other sources further attribute this mitzva to the fear that if converts are not loved, they might abandon Judaism to return to the
community that loves them. Some midrashim thus explain certain
rules as grounded in the concern "lest the convert return to their old
faith."[8] Even these sources, however, still recognize that the obligation to love the stranger in our midst is part of the legacy of Jewish
slavery in Egypt and of our having been *gerim* in that setting.[9]

Regardless of which concern is more paramount to a given reader
of this work, it is clear that there is a special obligation to act with
particular kindness to converts as a way of showing love. For example: the obligation includes a directive to help a convert celebrate
the festivals,[10] when they might feel most alone.[11] Furthermore:
according to many sources,[12] the Biblical repetition of the injunction
against oppressing a convert[13] reinforces the prohibition against oppressing the convert, both in financial matters and in non-financial
matters. Moreover, many halachic authorities are of the view that
there is even an obligation to help a convert earn a living with ease.[14]

2.   Arevut: Since a convert is basically viewed as identical to a born-
     Jew,[15] **converts can mutually participate with fellow Jews in**

---

8. This includes the same Midrash as the stag, Bamidbar Rabba 8:2.
9. Exodus 22:20 וְגֵר לֹא־תוֹנֶה וְלֹא תִלְחָצֶנּוּ כִּי־גֵרִים הֱיִיתֶם בְּאֶרֶץ מִצְרָיִם.
10. OC 529:2.
11. Dev 16:11.
12. See Sefer Hachinuch 63 and 64. See also Rambam Sefer Hamitzvot, mitzva 307.
13. Exodus 22:20 and 33:9.
14. See references in Sefer Hamitzvot of Rabbi Yerucham Perlow, Aseh 82.
15. Shemot 12:48 notes this explicitly. See also the Mechilta on this verse.

discharging religious obligations for each other even when they have already fulfilled their own obligation (called in Jewish law the principle of *arevut*).[16] Although this matter is in dispute, the general halachic consensus is that a convert can fulfill the obligation of others, even after they have fulfilled their own.[17] This work accepts that view.[18]

While there are many proofs for this approach, suffice it to say that this is the consensus of halachic authorities. It is also driven by the categorical insistence of many authorities that a convert may lead a congregation in prayer (be *motzi* others as *sheliach tzibbur*);[19] if a convert were not included in *arevut*, this rule of allowing a convert to be a *sheliach tzibbur/chazzan* would need many caveats and modifications. In addition, this approach is consistent with Rav Feinstein's obligation that we love the convert by being lenient on matters that could otherwise stigmatize them.

3. Minhagim: **A convert is free to choose which set of Jewish customs (*minhagim*) the convert wishes to adopt (Ashkenaz, Sephard, Edot Hamizrach, etc.).** A convert is under no obligation to adopt the customs of their biological homeland (so a Gentile born in Ukraine need not adopt minhag Ashkenaz) as long as the convert adopts an existent halachic culture.

The same point is true in matters of *hashkafa* (ideology): **A convert may choose any Orthodox ideology, spanning the breadth of the Orthodox community.**

Even if a convert's biological father is Jewish, the convert still

---

16. The principle of *arevut* (mutual responsibility) allows even people who have already fulfilled their obligation to facilitate others doing the same. Thus, the person who has already fulfilled a commandment can perform the commandment again on behalf of someone else, since the other person's obligation is really like their own. For example, a man who has already blown a *shofar* may blow a *shofar* again for one who has not yet heard the *shofar*. This, despite the guiding rule that only those who are currently obligated to the same degree can discharge on their behalf a specific obligation.

17. Tosafot, Niddah 13b; Panim Meirot 1:66.

18. OPG 192. The core of this dispute is between Peri Megadim General Introduction 2:16, where R. Yosef Teumim is uncertain whether converts are part of *arevut*, and his General Introduction, 3:29 where he rules that converts are indeed classified as part of *arevut*.

19. Shulchan Aruch OC 53:19.

need not adopt his father's ancestral family practices. Rabbi Shlomo
Zalman Auerbach does note that a convert should not adopt a mosaic
of unique customs from varied communities. Rather a convert should
choose a community to join,[20] and adopt that community's practices.[21]

4.   **"A convert is like a newborn child"** (*ger shenitgayer kekatan
     shenolad*): This principle is a limited one. It means only that a
     convert loses (from a Jewish law perspective) their biological and
     marital relationships with their prior Gentile family. As a matter
     of Jewish law, the convert technically has no mother, father, sib-
     lings, or spouse.[22]

This principle explains why a convert's halachic relationship with
their family is sometimes different than that of a born-Jew with
theirs. However, this principle has very limited application: an adult
convert is not "born again" at conversion. The convert does not have
to wait thirteen years to become a *bar-mitzva*, or twelve years to become a *bat-mitzva*. The convert has to repay any money that they
owed at the time of conversion, and continues to own any property
that they owned prior to their conversion. In short: the convert is not
a newborn child for most matters of Jewish law.

   These principles form the basis of many of the rules and decisions
found throughout this work, and are not necessarily repeated every
time that they are applicable.

Two Key Factors in Deciding Normative
Jewish Law (Halacha)

Most of the topics discussed in this work are drawn from disputes
by post-medieval rabbinic sages (*Achronim*),[23] by medieval sages
(*Rishonim*),[24] and even by sages in the Talmud itself. Thus, in order

---

   20. Rav Ovadia Yosef (*Yechave Daat* 5:33) indicates that a convert in Israel
ought to become Sephardi, but this limitation is not accepted by the Ashkenaz
community.
   21. *Halichot Shlomo, Moadim*, page 91 and OPG 156–158.
   22. See Rabbi Shaul Yisraeli, "A Convert is Like a Newborn Child," *Chavot
Binyamin* 2:67.
   23. Jewish law authorities after the year 1500.
   24. Jewish law authorities prior to 1500, but after the writing of the Talmud.

to reach practical conclusions, we have utilized two key factors to guide us.

FIRST KEY FACTOR:

This book's conclusions are reached through conventional analyses widely used for many halachic disputes, the details of which are beyond the scope of this introduction. The two of these guidelines relevant to this work are: Ashkenazi norm is generally followed when matters are disputed between Ashkenazim and Sephardim (although we also note Sephardic practice), and when the *Aruch Hashulchan* or *Mishnah Berurah* resolves a dispute, this work is inclined to follow their resolution over that of other *poskim* in that era.

SECOND KEY FACTOR:

We have always granted great weight to the obligation to love the convert. As Rav Moshe Feinstein states simply and directly,[25] this mitzva affects how one resolves halachic questions that affect a convert:

אבל למעשה יש לידע, שהמצווה של ואהבתם את הגר (דברים עקב י' י"ט) מחייבת אותנו לקרבם ולהקל בכל עניינים אלו.

But, as a matter of normative practice, one should know that the mitzva to love the convert (Devarim, Eikev, 10:19) obligates us to bring them closer and to be lenient on all these matters.

Rav Feinstein's approach mandates that where there is more than one reasonable approach to a matter of Jewish law concerning how to conduct oneself vis-a-vis a convert, one ought to adopt the approach that manifests love of the convert, and not draw prejudicial distinctions between the convert and the born-Jew. This pathway is both reasonable as a matter of normative halacha and at the same time enables fulfillment of the positive Torah obligation of loving the convert. That positive commandment rests its thumb on the halachic scales to encourage the resolution in a loving way. Ruling in a manner that stigmatizes the convert should only be done when that is the sole reasonable halachic option.

In other words, just as my teachers taught me, so does this respon-

---

25. See Igrot Moshe YD 4:26.

sum of Rav Feinstein teach us that the mitzva of loving the convert directs one to resolve halachic disputes about the proper conduct of a convert (or towards a convert) in the way that manifests the greatest love to the convert. We are definitely not to resolve such a dispute in a way that stigmatizes, shames, or humiliates a convert. The Torah obligation to love a convert is not an abstract duty to love. Rather, as Rav Feinstein notes, it creates an obligation to rule on matters of Jewish law in a way that allows the convert to sense that love and encourages others to manifest that love. This obligation is as real as the other specific obligations that Jewish law commands, such as the obligation to invite a convert for *Yom Tov* meals (above), or to allow a convert to serve as a Rosh Yeshiva (OC 529, CM 8).

קיצור שולחן ערוך לגרים

(על פי סדר השולחן ערוך)

A Concise Code of Jewish Law
for Converts

(in the order of the Shulchan Aruch)

This code follows the order of topics found in the four-sectioned Shulchan Aruch Code of Jewish Law. Each issue discussed is listed by the corresponding Shulchan Aruch section and chapter number. In addition to easing cross-referencing, this system allows readers to efficiently find topics once they are familiar with the basic organizational structure of the Shulchan Aruch – as outlined in the Listing of Topics on the following pages.

Listing of Topics in the Order Found in the Shulchan Aruch

Orach Chaim
Daily, Sabbath, and Holiday Laws

DAILY LAWS OF PRAYERS AND BLESSINGS

Yoreh Deah

**Kashrut • Idolatry • Loan Interest • *Nidda* • Vows • Honoring
One's Parents and the Elderly • Charity • Circumcision of Sons •
Conversion • Sacred Writings • Agrarian Living • Mourning**

Even Haezer

**Procreation, Permitted and Forbidden Marriage Partners •
Celebrating Weddings • Marital Obligations and Rights •
Divorce • Levirate Marriage and Release • Raped or Seduced Child**

Choshen Mishpat
Rabbinic Courts • Loans • Oppressing/Cheating/Overpricing •
Gifts *Causa Mortis* • Objects Lost and Found • Inheritance •
Paying Monies Owed

LAWS OF RABBINIC COURTS

CM 7:   Serving on a *Bet Din* for Monetary Matters
CM 8:   Discretionary Authority (*Serara*)
CM 26:   The Prohibition of Litigating in Secular Court
CM 33:   A Convert as a Witness
           A Convert's Credibility about Pre-Conversion Events
           Biologically Related Converts Witnessing and Testifying
CM 34:   Repentance from Pre-Conversion Sins in Order to Be a
           Valid Witness

LAWS OF LOAN DEBTS

CM 67:   The Sabbatical Year Cancellation of Loan Debts
CM 97:   The Sin of Pressuring or Even Pestering a Moneyless
           Convert to Repay a Loan

LAWS OF OPPRESSING, CHEATING AND OVERPRICING

CM 228:   The Sin of Cheating or Tormenting a Convert
           The Obligation to Repay the Differential, or to Cancel,
           Overpriced Sales

LAWS OF GIFTING

CM 256:   Gifts *Causa Mortis* (in Anticipation of Death)

LAWS OF OBJECTS LOST AND FOUND

CM 259:   Property That a Convert Found or Lost as a Gentile
CM 270:   Property That a Child-Convert Found

LAWS OF INHERITANCE

CM 277:   Inheritance of the First Son Born after the Father's
           Conversion

Orach Chaim

Daily, Sabbath, and Holiday Laws

Daily Laws of Prayers and Blessings

OC 6: VARIANT PRAYER CUSTOMS

Since there are communal variations in prayer texts (*nusach*) and in other prayer-related customs, a convert may theoretically adopt those of any community they wish, as long as they remain loyal and consistent within this choice. However, if one converts in a place with a well-established prayer text (*nusach*) and collective set of customs (*minhagim*), then the convert must adhere to those.[1] (Generally, a convert should have thought about this issue prior to conversion and should have a community in mind to join with its customs.)

OC 25: DONNING *TEFILLIN* AFTER CONVERSION

When a convert becomes Jewish, they are subject only to those commandments which are in effect at the time of the conversion. However, even if the convert has already performed such a commandment that day as a Gentile, the convert must repeat it in order to fulfill their obligation as a Jew.[2] Therefore: inasmuch as the time frame for donning *tefillin* is the entire day, a *ger* who converts in the afternoon must don *tefillin* (again, if done already prior to the conversion).

---

1. See Tefilla K'hilchata 4:5 in the name of many authorities and Halichot Shlomo 85 n. 80 and MhG, 171. See also Yabia Omer, OC 10:9; Yechave Da'at 5:33; Yalkut Yosef, OC 453:14 and YD 242:30, who claims that anyone converting in the Land of Israel must follow Sephardic custom.

2. Taz, YD 396:2 as explained by Machaneh Efraim, EH 3:66. MhG, pp. 183–184 and OPG 239.

OC 39: THE VALIDITY OF *TEFILLIN* WRITTEN BY SOMEONE WHO REVERTS TO THEIR OLD FAITH OUT OF FEAR

A convert can work as a *sofer stam* (religious scribe), and all their work is valid to the same degree as that of a born-Jew. There are those who claim that a convert who apostatizes out of fear of governmental authorities can write a valid *sefer torah*, *tefillin*, and *mezuzot*.[3] Since the convert is rejecting the faith only in order to save their life, the convert is viewed as a full-fledged Jew. (Furthermore: there are many who claim that the rules regarding a convert who had reverted to their faith of birth are more lenient than for a born-Jew who had converted out of fear of death.[4])

OC 46: THE BLESSING OF "*SHELO ASANI GOY*"

There is a dispute regarding what blessing a convert should direct to God while born-Jews bless God for not having been made a Gentile.[5] Although there are a number of prayers in which the convert lays claim to historical membership in the Jewish people (see OC 60), this blessing can be viewed as different since blessing God in the morning for "not making me a Gentile" would appear to be a false statement in the first person. Accordingly, some Sephardic *poskim* suggest that the convert skip the blessing while some Ashkenazic *poskim* suggest that the convert modify the wording appropriately.[6] However, due to the mitzva to love a convert as a fully-included member of the Jewish

---

3. Beit Yosef, OC 39:3; OC 39:3; YD 281:2. But see Aruch Hashulchan, OC 39:3, who states simply, "Regarding a convert who reverted to his faith due to a fear of persecution – the Rosh, Tur, and Shulchan Aruch ruled that he is qualified to write. But from the Tosfot in Gittin it does not appear to be true. So too, the Rif and Rambam do note cite it. Therefore, one should not be lenient." See also Mishna Berura 39:11, which seems to validate *tefillin* written by a non-observant convert who is in a situation of danger to life. See also *Teshuvot V'hanhagot* 3:309–310.

4. See the previous footnote.

5. Beit Yosef, OC 46:4; Bach, OC 46:7; Rema, OC 46:4; Taz, OC 46:5; Pri Chadash, OC 47:5; Darchei Moshe, OC 46:3; Mishnah Berura 46:18; Yalkut Yosef, OC 46:21; Abudraham, Morning Blessings s.v. *kesheshomeia kol.*

6. This topic is the subject of the essay by Michael Broyde and Mark Goldfeder, "*Shelo Asani Goy*: What Bracha Does a *Ger* Bless?" (see Supplemental Essay A), which discusses the many approaches to this problem, ranging from the view that the convert makes the blessing *sheasani yisrael* through the view that the convert skips the *bracha* and to the view that the convert make a different blessing entirely.

people, the preferred ruling is that of the Rambam and the kabbalists, who rule that a convert may bless God as all do[7] – although Sephardi *poskim* are more insistent that the convert omit God's name in this blessing.[8]

OC 47: THE BLESSING OF *"ASHER BACHAR BANU MIKOL AM"*

As a Jew, a convert blesses God for having chosen the Jews as the recipients of the Torah (*asher bachar banu mikol am*[9]).[10] Although there are authorities who rule that converts should not recite this phrase, common custom and contemporary rabbinic consensus rule that converts should recite these words.[11]

OC 47: BLESSING GOD FOR THE TORAH

Since the requirement to bless God for the Torah applies all day until one actually thanks God, on day one, a convert should say *birchat hatorah* after converting,[12] before studying Torah.[13]

OC 53: LEADING CONGREGATIONAL PRAYERS (*CHAZZAN*)

A convert may represent the congregation before God, and may serve as *shaliach tzibbur*[14] to discharge obligations for others. Although some authorities question the convert's ability to state that God is the "God of our Fathers," *elokei avoteinu*, normative practice is that converts recite all such phrases. Furthermore: although there is some question whether a convert can discharge others of Biblical obligations, such as blowing the *shofar* and chanting the special *parshat*

---

7. This is the view of Rabbi Mordechai Willig.

8. KhG 52 at page 119 and note 52.

9. "Who selected us from all the other nations."

10. Magen Avraham 47:3; Shulchan Aruch Harav, OC 47:4; Mishna Berura 47:8; KhG 58 at page 126.

11. This topic is discussed in the first supplemental essay.

12. Yalkut Yosef, OC 47:34.

13. KhG 57 at page 126. This is logical as it is a blessing applicable all day.

14. Sefer Ha'agur, Hilchot Berachot 91; Beit Yosef, OC 53:19; OC 53:19; Levush, 53:19, Magen Avraham 53:19; Eishel Avraham, OC 53:19; Yalkut Yosef, OC 53:20. KhG 55 at page 122.

zachor reading, common custom is to allow converts to discharge fellow Jews of any such obligations.[15]

OC 55: BEING COUNTED TOWARDS A QUORUM (*MINYAN*)

A *ger* counts towards a prayer quorum of ten men (a *minyan*).[16] The convert also counts towards a quorum of Jews in front of whom one must avoid desecrating God's name even at the cost of sacrificing one's life (*venikdashti betoch bnei yisrael*).[17]

OC 60: THE WORDS OF "*U-VANU BACHARTA*" IN THE BLESSING PRECEDING *SHEMA*

As a Jew, a convert also lists God's having chosen to love the Jews (*u-vanu bacharta*) when blessing God for His love immediately before reciting the Biblical *Shema* passage.[18] Although there are authorities who rule that converts should not recite this phrase, common custom and contemporary rabbinic consensus rule that converts should recite these words in both individual and group prayer.[19]

OC 62: *SHEMA* AND PRAYER IN THE VERNACULAR

If necessary, any Jew, including one converted, may recite *Shema*, pray, or bless in their vernacular.[20]

OC 111: BLESSING GOD AFTER *SHEMA* FOR TAKING OUR ANCESTORS OUT OF EGYPT

A convert recites all parts of the prayer service that relate to our ancestors' Exodus from Egypt.[21] Although a convert's biological ances-

---

15. OPG 192; but see MHG 168–169, who questions this. I am inclined here not to rule stringently.

16. OC 55:1 (by implication). Eishel Avraham, OC 55:4 makes this clear. KhG 54 states this explicitly.

17. OPG 233 and sources cited there. But see Pitchei Teshuva, YD 157:7. In contrast see Tosfot, Sukka 28b sv *l'rabot*.

18. Magen Avraham 47:3; Shulchan Aruch Harav, OC 47:4; Mishna Berura 47:8; KhG 58 at page 126.

19. This topic is discussed in Supplemental Essay A.

20. OC 62:2 and Mekor Chaim 62:2.

21. Teshuvot Harambam 293 cited infra in note 23.

tors did not take part in the Exodus, a convert has become a part of the history of the Jewish people whom God has saved miraculously.[22]

OC 113: BLESSING GOD AS GOD OF OUR FOREFATHERS

A convert blesses God as *eloheinu ve'elohei avoteinu*.[23] Although some early authorities discourage this as inaccurate, Rambam rules that a convert should say all such wordings, and that is the common custom. See entry OC 47.

OC 116: PRAYING FOR ONE'S GENTILE PARENTS' HEALTH

A convert may pray for the recovery of their Gentile parents, one's father and mother who brought them into this world.[24] (Indeed, Jews may pray for the recovery of any Gentile.[25])

OC 135: A CONVERT CANNOT BE A KOHEN OR LEVI

A biological son of a Kohen or Levi who converts is never classified as a Kohen or Levi and thus does not receive honors as such, since he never inherits or receives his biological father's status.[26] Related to this is the rule that a convert does not inherit from his father regardless of whether his father is Gentile or Jewish. See entry CM 283.

OC 139: CALLING A CONVERT UP TO THE TORAH (AN *ALIYA*)

A *ger* is called up to the Torah as *ben Avraham* instead of *ben Avraham avinu* so as not to call attention to his conversion.[27] Alternatively, he may be called up as *ben* [his natural father's name in the vernacular]. According to Rav Bentzion Uziel, the children of a *ger* who

---

22. Rambam's Letter to Ovadia Hager as found in Teshuvot Harambam 293.
23. Tosfot, Bava Batra 81a; Teshuvot Harambam 293; Kaf Hachaim, OC 113:1.
24. Yechave Da'at 6:60; Yalkut Yosef, YD 1:30; KhG 60 at page 127.
25. Although such prayers are usually said using the Hebrew name of the sick person and the Hebrew name of their mother, it may be said using any name by which the sick person is known.
26. Yalkut Yosef, OC 135:8.
27. Rema, OC 139:3; Aruch Hashulchan, OC 139:6. A convert who wishes to be called up as *ben Avraham avinu* should be called up as such. See Keter Shem Tov 1:332–335 and the sources cited therein, who even notes that this is most proper. See KhG 41 at page 98.

converted along with their father may even be called up with their father's Jewish name.[28] Common custom, however, is that they too are referred to as *ben Avraham*. The same ruling obtains any time a *giyoret* uses her Hebrew name and the name of her mother socially.

OC 141: CALLING BROTHER CONVERTS UP TO THE TORAH IN SUCCESSION

Although immediate relatives are not called up for *aliyot* in succession, biologically related converts may be called up for successive *aliyot*.[29] This should not be done, however, if the converts are likely to be insulted.

OC 166: *BIRKAT HAMAZON* AFTER CONVERSION

One who eats bread before immersing in a *mikva* to convert is not obligated after the conversion to bless God with *birkat hamazon*. This is because a convert is as a newborn.[30]

OC 187: THE SECOND BLESSING OF *BIRKAT HAMAZON*

Although some disagree, a convert says the words "that you granted our fathers" (*she-hinchalta la-avoteinu*) whenever one recites *birkat hamazon*.[31]

OC 199, 201: BLESSING *BIRKAT HAMAZON* AS A GROUP (*ZIMMUN*)

A convert can join or lead a group (a *zimmun*) that is blessing God for food eaten (*birkat hamazon*).[32] In general, converts can mutually participate with fellow Jews in discharging religious obligations (*arevut*)

---

28. Mishpetei Uziel, YD 2:59. I have been told that Rabbi Moshe Feinstein also allowed this.

29. MHG 250.

30. MHG 164. See Rabbi Akiva Eiger to OC 186 for a discussion similar to this.

31. Tosfot, Bava Batra 81a; Tur, OC 199; Beit Yosef, OC 199:4; Bach, OC 199:3–4; OC 199:4; Mishbetzot Zahav, OC 199:1; Eishel Avraham, OC 186:1; Mishnah Berura 199:6, 7.

32. Tosfot, Bava Batra 81a; Beit Yosef, OC 199:4; Perisha, OC 186:1; Bach, OC 199:3–4; OC 199:4; Panim Meirot 1:66.

and can even lead (be *motzi* others).[33] These issues relate to the ones discussed above in entries OC 53 and OC 113.

OC 232: THE AFTERNOON PRAYER (*MINCHA*) AFTER CONVERSION

Ideally, one who converts in the afternoon should not eat before praying the afternoon *mincha* that day, just as one is forbidden to eat on any day before praying (first thing in the morning).[34]

OC 235: RECITING NIGHTTIME *SHEMA* AFTER COMPLETING CONVERSION AT NIGHT

Inasmuch as the time frame for nightly prayer and for nightly recitation of the Biblical *Shema* passage extends through the night, someone who converts at night is equal to others in their obligation to pray *ma'ariv* as well as to recite *Shema*.[35]

Sabbath Laws

OC 261: CONVERSION AFTER SHABBAT COMMENCES

Conversions may not be done on a Day of Rest (Shabbat or festivals).[36] Nonetheless, if one did convert on Shabbat, the consensus of the authorities in this after-the-fact case is that the convert is fully obligated to observe the remainder of Shabbat in spite of not having been obligated at its commencement.[37]

OC 294: *HAVDALAH* AFTER CONVERTING ON SATURDAY NIGHT

Even if one converted immediately after Shabbat, one is not obligated to bless over ending Shabbat (*havdalah*) since there is no obligation of *havdalah* for a Shabbat one was not obligated to observe.[38]

---

33. Tosfot, Kiddushin 70b; Harei Besamim 1:28.
34. MHG 164.
35. Magen Avraham 687 (intro) and Levush Mordechai 19.
36. Like any other court activity: CM 5.
37. Yeshuot Yaakov 608:1; Chazon Nachum 1:89; B'tzel Hachochma 1:52.
38. Hanhagot U'psakim Rav Yosef Chaim Sonnenfeld, Mekorot U'tziyunim,

OC 370: THE EFFECT OF A SHABBAT CONVERSION ON AN *ERUV*

The Jerusalem Talmud[39] notes that one who improperly converted on Shabbat morning after dawn "acquires a residency" that then interferes with the shared neighborhood (*eruv*) of permitted carrying that was set up before Shabbat.[40] Thus, the convert would have to cancel their right to carry in the area in order to allow everyone else to carry in the area in the case of such an *eruv*.[41]

Holiday and Festival Laws

OC 423: PRAYING MUSSAF AFTER CONVERTING ON ROSH CHODESH

One who converts during the daytime of Rosh Chodesh needs to pray the additional (*mussaf*) Rosh Chodesh prayer (*amidah*) since its time frame extends to the end of the day.[42]

OC 431: SEARCHING FOR *CHAMETZ* AFTER CONVERTING DURING THE DAY BEFORE PESACH

One who converts on *erev Pesach* is obligated to search for *chametz* and destroy it just like anyone else who for some reason did not search on the preceding eve.

OC 432: EREV PESACH FAST OF THE FIRSTBORN

A convert who is a firstborn[43] does not have to observe the fast of the

---

Hilchot Havdala, note 10 (as found in Bar Ilan 22+ though missing from print editions).

39. Jerusalem Talmud, Eruvin 4:5.

40. It is hard to determine if this Yerushalmi passage is halachically binding since it is not codified in the Shulchan Aruch and there are no traditions regarding this, especially inasmuch as conversions simply do not take place on Shabbat.

41. Mishna Eruvin 6:3–4; Rambam MT Eruvin 2:1; Shulchan Aruch OH 371:5; AH and MB there.

42. See OC 25.

43. This includes a convert who is the biological child of a Jewish father, boy or girl.

firstborn[44] nor attend a religious festive meal (*siyum*) in order to be excused from fasting.[45]

OC 446: REMOVING *CHAMETZ* BEFORE CONVERTING ON PESACH

One who converts on Pesach should ensure that one has no *chametz* in their possession so that they do not, upon conversion, immediately transgress the prohibition against owning *chametz*.[46]

OC 473: *HAGGADA* REFERENCES TO OUR AND OUR FOREFATHERS' EXODUS

A convert recites all the historical passages of the *haggada*[47] in line with the general approach that a convert has joined the historical narrative of the Jewish people. See entries above OC 47 and OC 53.

OC 489: COUNTING THE *OMER* AFTER CONVERSION

Since the mitzva of counting forty-nine days from the Pesach date of the ancient offering of an *omer* of barley to the Shavuot date of the ancient wheat offering (*sefirat ha'omer*) is a protracted mitzva, one who converts in this period encounters the classical dispute among the authorities as to whether someone who has not counted all the days from the beginning does or not does not count *sefira* with a blessing. This is because, as a newborn Jew, he did not count from the beginning.[48] Accordingly, some authorities rule that only if one converts on the first day of *sefirat ha'omer* can one continue counting the *omer* with a blessing.[49] Others, however, insist that a convert is no different than one who becomes an adult (*bar* or *bat mitzva*)

---

44. Shevet Halevi 8:117. However, he notes that it is ideal to be strict since if the convert had converted back in Egypt, he would have been saved along with all the other Jewish firstborn. Cf. *Haseder Ha'aruch*, Vol. 3, p. 44.

45. But KhG 66 at page 135 encourages participation in a *siyum*.

46. SGK p. 63. If he converts and has *chametz* in his possession, he is like any Jew who discovers *chametz* on Pesach. See OC 435:1, 446, and 447. See also Machane Chaim, OC 3:32 for a relevant discussion.

47. Birkei Yosef, OC 473:17; Sha'arei Teshuva, OC 473:27.

48. Birkei Yosef, OC 489:20; Aruch Hashulchan, OC 489:1, 15; Ktav Sofer, OC 99; Chelkat Yaakov, OC 206; Har Tzvi 2:76; Tzitz Eliezer 14:55; Sha'arei Teshuva, OC 489; KhG at 67.

49. Birkei Yosef, OC 489:21.

during this time – who counts with a blessing as long as one has been counting from the beginning as a minor. In light of this debate, some recommend that a Gentile who expects to convert during the *omer* period not count the *omer* at all while still a Gentile so that they should not become doubtfully obligated to count with a blessing upon conversion.[50] This writer is of the view that a convert should always count with a blessing, just like a *bar mitzva* youth.

OC 490: BLESSING *SHEHECHEYANU* AFTER CONVERTING ON *CHOL HAMO'ED*

Although one who forgot to bless God at the beginning of a holiday for having lived to celebrate it can bless *shehecheyanu* whenever one recalls to do so during the weekdays (*chol hamo'ed*) of the festival,[51] the *poskim* debate whether one who converts on *chol hamo'ed* and did not experience the holiday of the festival as a Jew should bless *shehecheyanu* in honor of the festival. Some suggest that the convert make the blessing on a new fruit or garment and have in mind the Yom Tov as well. Others rule that an independent *shehecheyanu* blessing in honor of the festival is justified.[52] Logic inclines one to suggest that the *shehecheyanu* blessing should indeed be recited in honor of the holiday with its celebrations and its ongoing mitzvot that the convert performs for the first time as a Jew.[53]

OC 496: NO OBSERVANCE OF A SECOND DAY OF YOM TOV BY A FOREIGNER WHO CONVERTS IN ISRAEL

A person from abroad who converts in Israel and is still residing in Israel observes only one day of Yom Tov holiday instead of the two days observed by the Jews of the diaspora. This is true during their time in Israel even if they will be returning to live in the Diaspora.[54]

---

50. OPG 241.

51. See for example: Shulchan Aruch haRav OH 473:3 and 643:5.

52. MHG 167.

53. The *shehecheyanu* blessing of Yom Tov relates to both the mitzvot of the Yom Tov as well as to the holiness of the day (SGK 63–64).

54. B'tzel Hachochma 1:36 and MHG 165. Although others disagree, there are additional reasons to rule this way nowadays.

OC 529: THE OBLIGATION OF FELLOW JEWS TO HELP THE CONVERT REJOICE ON YOM TOV

Fellow Jews have a special obligation to feast with converts on Yom Tov since holidays are a time when a convert is likely to feel most alone.[55]

OC 566: CONVERSION ON A FAST DAY

One who converts on a fast day should start fasting from the beginning, even before the conversion, so that one can fulfill the obligation to be fasting to the appropriate degree at the time that one emerges from the *mikva*.[56] This suggests to some authorities that one who ate before conversion need not bother fasting.[57] However, inasmuch as eating and drinking on a fast day are sinful in and of themselves each time one does so even if one has already eaten or drunk,[58] some rule that even the convert who ate earlier must join the fast after conversion.[59] In any case, wine clearly should not be used when the convert is named on a fast day – unless it will be given to someone who is permitted to drink wine that day.[60]

CONVERSION ON A POSTPONED FAST DAY (*TAANIT NIDCHE*)

There is some discussion whether one who converts on a minor fast day that, due to Shabbat, was postponed from its official date (*taanit nidche*) is required to fast with everyone else. This is because one could argue that a person who wasn't Jewish on the official date of the fast never became obligated to fast.[61] However, even if we put the

---

55. OC 529:2. In addition: this obligation parallels the halachic prohibition of inviting a Gentile for the Yom Tov meals (OC 512). The convert must be invited to celebrate together because he is truly Jewish.

56. See Ha'emek Sheila 167:6. Cf. Chashukei Chemed, Bava Kama 83a who argues that there is no such thing as a partial fast day and Yeshuot Yaakov OC 608:1 who notes the same for Yom Kippur.

57. Rabbi Ari Enkin adds that the rule for Temple times that a convert brings and eats a sacrifice on the day of conversion further suggests that a convert is not required to fast on the day that he converts.

58. See for example: Shu"T Binyan Tzion 34.

59. See for example: Meshekh Chokhma, Emor 23:29 as regards Yom Kippur.

60. For a discussion of the conditions under which someone might drink wine on a fast day, see Shu"T Lehorot Natan 2:36.

61. Avnei Nezer, OC 426; Mishnat Hager p. 167.

complicated discussion of the status of a *taanit nidche* aside as beyond the scope of this work, the mitzva of "you shall love the convert" suggests that a convert should fast with everyone else. Since allowing the convert to observe as all do is generally what the convert wishes, it manifests love.

CONVERSION ON SUNDAY THE 10TH AV (TISHA B'AV *NIDCHE*)

When one converts on Sunday the 10th of Av (a Sunday on which the fast of 9th Av is observed instead of on Shabbat), there is even more reason to fast. This is because that Sunday, the 10th of Av, more than being a mere fast postponed (from its original date on which the convert had not yet been Jewish and obligated), might have the status of an actual fast date inasmuch as the 10th of Av was one of the days during which the Temple had been destroyed (and so the convert is undoubtedly obligated).[62]

OC 589: LEADING SERVICES AND BLOWING *SHOFAR* ON ROSH HASHANA

A *ger* may lead a congregation in High Holiday prayers and blow the New Year *shofar* horn for his fellow Jews[63] since converts can mutually participate with fellow Jews in discharging religious obligations (*arevut*). See OC 199 above.

OC 612: FASTING AFTER A YOM KIPPUR CONVERSION

Inasmuch as the Day of Atonement requires fasting for a full day from the preceding evening,[64] it is possible to argue that someone who converts on Yom Kippur (improperly *a priori*[65]) does not have to complete the fast in which one was not obligated before conversion. However, inasmuch as eating and drinking on Yom Kippur are sinful

---

62. See Avnei Nezer, OC 426 who discusses the nature of the fast of Sunday 10 Av. Teshuvot Harashba 1:520 argues that 9 Av carries no special weight when it falls out on Shabbat and that 10 Av becomes the actual fast day. Since Rema 553:2 applies some strictures to Shabbat 9 Av, he implicitly disagrees with the Rashba's assessment of Sunday 10 Av. However, there is reason to suggest otherwise as the basic status of Shabbat 9 Av is in contest.
63. Teshuvot V'hanhagot 1:342, 3:162.
64. Yeshuot Yaakov 608:1 and Har Tzvi OC 1:155.
65. See OC 261 above.

in and of themselves each time one does so, even if one has already eaten or drunk,[66] some authorities require the convert to fast anyway after conversion.[67] Some further argue that, inasmuch as there is an obligation to suffer the date in hunger and thirst (and not only a sin to eat or drink),[68] the convert will need to have fasted from the beginning of Yom Kippur before they had converted in order to avoid inherently violating this obligation to suffer once they become a Jew.[69]

OC 637, 641: DWELLING IN A *SUKKAH* AFTER CONVERTING ON SUKKOT

One who converts after the opening Yom Tov of Sukkot must fulfill the mitzva of dwelling in a *sukkah* for the remainder of the holiday and must do so with a blessing – in spite of the fact that one inherently cannot become obligated on that holiday to dwell in a *sukkah* for all seven days[70] as the Torah mandates.[71] In addition, similar to anyone who could not be in a *sukkah* at the beginning of Sukkot, the convert blesses the *shehecheyanu* blessing of gratitude the first time they sit down to dwell in a *sukkah*.[72] Moreover, although unnecessary work is forbidden on the weekdays of the Feasts, the convert may build a *sukkah* if they lack one, just as any other Jew who needs to do so may build one.[73]

OC 649, 658: FULFILLING THE OBLIGATION OF THE FIRST DAY OF SUKKOT TO LIFT UP FOUR SPECIES THAT ONE OWNS

Because the acquisitions of a Gentile remain in force even after conversion, a convert may fulfill the mitzva of lifting up cuttings of four species of plants (*arba minim*) with the selections that were acquired before converting. Nevertheless, some say that it is preferable for the convert to first make an additional act of acquisition, through picking

---

66. See for example: Shu"T Binyan Tzion 34.
67. See for example: Meshekh Chokhma, Emor 23:29 as regards Yom Kippur.
68. Mishna Keritut 1:1; Rambam MT Shevitat Asor 1:4.
69. See Ha'emek Sheila 167:6.
70. Birkei Yosef, OC 637:1, Aruch Hashulchan, OC 637:1; Mishna Berura 637:2; Maharsham 2:65; Avnei Nezer, OC 504; Mishpetei Uziel, OC 3:73.
71. Leviticus 23:42.
72. Yalkut Yosef, OC 637:2.
73. Sh"A OC 637:1.

them up with intent to acquire, before lifting them up for the Sukkot celebrations and prayer.[74]

OC 662: FULFILLING THE OBLIGATION OF LIFTING UP FOUR SPECIES AFTER CONVERTING ON SUKKOT

One who converted during the weekdays of Sukkot (*chol hamo'ed*) must lift up the selections of the four species of plants on the remaining days, in spite of missing the critical Yom Tov lifting up. The convert even blesses the *shehecheyanu* blessing of gratitude the first time one does so.[75]

OC 671: LIGHTING CHANUKA CANDLES AFTER CONVERTING DURING CHANUKA

One who converts during Chanuka lights the candles on the remaining nights according to the day of the holiday, since on every night there is an independent mitzva to commemorate the miracle again.[76] A convert also blesses *shehecheyanu* the first time they light Chanuka candles, similar to any Jew who missed the initial lightings.

OC 676: CHANUKA PRAYERS

A convert can praise God for having performed miracles for our forefathers (*she'asa nisim la'avoteinu*) on Chanuka and whenever else such praise is recited – just as the convert prays to God as God of our forefathers (*elokeinu v'elokei avoteinu*).[77] See above entry OC 53.

OC 685: *PARSHAT ZACHOR*

As a member of the historical narrative of the Jewish people, a convert has an obligation to recite or hear *Parshat Zachor*, and counts toward a quorum (*minyan*) for the reading.[78] Cf. entries OC 47 and OC 60.

---

74. Machaneh Chaim 3:31 and MHG. 165.
75. Cf. Mishnah Berurah 662:3.
76. Chochmat Shlomo, OC 677:2; B'tzel Hachochma 1:52; Yalkut Yosef, OC 677:7; MHG 165.
77. Pri Chadash, OC 676:1; Eliyah Rabba, OC 676:2; Eishel Avraham, OC 675:4; Mishna Berura 675:14; KhG 59 at page 126.
78. B'tzel Hachochma 6:49; Sdei Chemed 3:67.

OC 687: EARLY PURIM MORNING CONVERSION

One who converts Purim morning after dawn but before sunrise is not obligated in the previous nighttime's reading of *Megillat Esther*.[79] However, the convert is obligated in the daytime *megilla* reading, as they were a Jew by the time the obligation became activated (sunrise).

PURIM DAY CONVERSION

In spite of its reading being allowed all day, there is a dispute whether one who converts during Purim day is obligated to read the *megilla*. This dispute is based on halacha's assigning each person their proper Purim date (Adar 14 or Adar 15) based on their location at sunrise on Adar 14.[80] Thus, although a convert should be obliged to read, both due to the fact that the reading obligation exists the entire day (as in entry OC 25) and that one can be assigned the default date of Adar 14, the convert preferably should avoid the question that year by *hearing* the *megilla* and its blessings, instead of reading it and blessing God directly.

CONVERTING IN JERUSALEM OVER A THREE-DAY PURIM WEEKEND (PURIM *MESHULASH*)

As regards someone who converts in Jerusalem over a three-day Purim weekend (*Purim Meshulash*), when the city's Adar 15 Shushan Purim falls out on Shabbat:[81] It seems clear that if one converts on Sunday, one is not obligated in any of the mitzvot of Purim since one missed the holiday date, and that if one converts on Friday, one is obligated in all of them, since one is Jewish by the time the holiday begins. If one converts on Shabbat during the daytime, a question similar to the one discussed in the previous paragraph arises, but the

---

79. Magen Avraham 687 (introduction); Eishel Avraham 687 (introduction); Machatzit Hashekel, OC 687 (introduction); Or Zarua 2; Hilchot Megilla no. 369. But see SGK 66 and Chelkat Yoav, OC 33.

80. Jerusalem Talmud, Megilla 2:3; Yad Eliyahu 93; Minchat Shlomo 1:23; Aruch Hashulchan, OC 687:4, MH p. 166; Chazon Ish, OC 152:3. This might depend on whether a person who is exempt from one reading is exempt from both readings.

81. In such a situation, some aspects of Purim are observed on Friday, some on Shabbat, and some on Sunday (MHG 166).

question has little relevance in practice since conversions are prohibited on Shabbat.

GOING TO JERUSALEM ON SHUSHAN PURIM AFTER CONVERTING ON PURIM

One who converts on Purim afternoon, so that one's obligation to read on Adar 14 is debated, and then goes to Jerusalem (the city that indubitably is obligated to celebrate Shushan Purim Adar 15) might be subject to special rules.[82]

OC 689, 692: OBLIGATION TO READ THE MEGILLAH

A convert is obligated to read *Megillat Esther* with its blessings just as one is obligated in all mitzvot that commemorate national historical events.[83] See earlier entries OC 47 and OC 60.

---

82. There is a doubt as to when one really needs to observe Purim in such a situation. Minchat Shlomo 1:23.

83. Birkei Yosef, OC 689:2; Sho'el U'meishiv, second edition, 3:109.

Yoreh Deah

Kashrut • Idolatry • Loan Interest • *Nidda* • Vows • Honoring
One's Parents and the Elderly • Charity • Circumcision of Sons •
Conversion • Sacred Writings • Agrarian Living • Mourning

Laws of *Kashrut* and Idolatry

YD 2: SLAUGHTER (*SHECHITA*) BY A CONVERT WHO REVERTS TO THEIR PRIOR FAITH

A convert is trusted and allowed to ritually slaughter (*shechita*), as any other Jew is allowed and trusted. A convert who abandons Judaism out of fear for their life is still trusted to slaughter an animal according to halacha's humane standards.[1] This is because most authorities rule that a convert who reverts to their prior faith out of fear is treated more leniently than a Jew who apostatizes out of fear. See CM 228.[2]

SLAUGHTER (*SHECHITA*) BY A CONVERT WHO CEASES TO OBSERVE ONE LAW

A convert who had validly converted as a fully observant Jew but later has become lax in one or more laws, remains Jewish,[3] and so their *shechita* is still trusted as long as the convert observes the rules of slaughtering an animal, monotheism, and Shabbat.[4]

---

1. YD 119:9.
2. Cf. OC 39 and GvG 49. The counterargument (that a convert apostate is no different than any other apostate) is found in Aruch Hashulchan, OC 39:3 as regards such a convert writing *tefillin*.
3. Bechorot 30b.
4. Bechorot 30b.

YD 61: PRIESTLY GIFTS AFTER CONVERTING

After slaughtering an animal, certain portions of the meat ought to be gifted to a Kohen, especially in Israel. A convert's obligation to give *matnot kehuna* from one's animal depends on the animal having been slaughtered after the conversion. In a case of doubt, one is not required to give these gifts of the *zeroa, lechayayim, v'keivah* (the fore-leg, the jaws, and the maw) to any Kohanim since the latter cannot prove their right to these gifts (*hamotzi m'chaveiro alav hara'aya*).[5]

YD 113: THE FOOD COOKED BY A GENTILE BEFORE CONVERSION (*BISHUL AKUM*)

The Talmudic Rabbis enacted a decree that prohibited a Jew from eating most foods cooked by a Gentile alone. However, a convert may eat any food that they cooked before the conversion. Some authorities argue that this is permitted because it is inherently impossible for the concerns of intermarriage, and of hidden non-kosher ingredients, to apply.[6] Others disagree. They are of the opinion that, although the decree against *bishul akum* applies regardless of the degree to which the underlying concerns are realistic or even inherently possible, this decree does not include food prepared by a person themself. According to the last approach, other Jews would be forbidden to eat the food.[7] In light of the mitzva to love the convert, it is best to permit anyone to eat the food.[8]

YD 120: IMMERSION OF UTENSILS

In general, a Jew must immerse any metal and glass food utensils purchased from or through a Gentile in a *mikva*, with a blessing. Thus, a convert who immersed and converted should also immerse

---

5. Chullin 134a-b; Tur, YD 61; YD 61:33, Aruch Hashulchan, YD 61:19. See also Taz, YD 268:16.

6. Food cooked by a Gentile. MHG p. 175.

7. This is against the reasoning of the MHG, who claims that the two underlying concerns do not apply in this case. On its face, the MHG would also permit others to eat this food, whereas the rationale present above would permit only the convert himself to partake in it.

8. Based on the view that once the person is Jewish, the prohibition to eat the food disappears. As noted by MHG p. 175.

their utensils with a blessing.[9] Others disagree and rule that utensils
that have been the valid utensils of someone who is now Jewish do
not require immersion.[10] Although the first view makes more sense, a
convert ought to immerse these utensils, but without a blessing with
God's name, since a number of authorities rule that no immersion
is needed.[11] Alternatively, the convert should purchase a utensil that
requires immersion with a blessing and immerse all of their utensils
at the same time. Rabbi Yitzchak Yosef proposes a further compromise: metal utensils, which require immersion as a matter of biblical
law, should be immersed without a blessing, while glass utensils,
which require immersion only as a matter of rabbinic law, need not
be immersed.[12]

The most logical explanation of the view that one need not immerse utensils upon conversion is found in the writings of Rabbi
Asher Weiss,[13] who presents two competing arguments in favor of
non-immersion of utensils. First, however, he concedes that most
halachic authorities agree that immersion is required. He states:

> In truth, I repeat that I know that most great and wonderful halachic
> authorities agree that a convert needs to immerse his untensils. Such I
> heard from the lips of Rabbi Yosef Shalom Elyashiv shlita, and Rabbi
> Chaim Kanefsky shlita and such is written in Shevat haLevi (4:92) and
> Teshuvot Vehanhagot (1:249) who all state that the convert immerses
> with a *bracha*; see there.

Rabbi Weiss then notes his disagreement based on silent precedent:

> However, I have always felt in my heart, now and in the past, that since
> we have not seen this halacha cited in the *Rishonim* and the *poskim* of

---

9. See Tzemach Yehuda 4:13; Tzitz Eliezer 8:19–20, 22:49; Shevet Halevi 4:92,
6:245; Yabia Omer 7:8; Avnei Nezer, YD 1:109; Teshuvot V'hanhagot 1:449;
Chadrei Deah, YD 120. It is widely reported that Rabbi Moshe Feinstein was
also of that view. There is a view that no blessing is recited, as the utensils are not
acquired from a Gentile. See GvG 49.

10. See Tzitz Eliezer 8:19–20, 22:49. So too, the Chassidic masters teach that
when a Gentile converts, his utensils "convert" with him and therefore need not
be immersed. See Shem Mishmuel, Drasha for Sukkot, 5677, page 158, KhG.

11. Tzitz Eliezer 8:19–20, 22:49; GvG 49.

12. KhG 63 at page 129–130. This approach is more consistent with two
Sephardic preferences: to be more strict about reciting blessings in vain and to
treat glass as different from metal for many Jewish law matters.

13. http://www.torahbase.org under the listing for parshat Matot.

the prior generations, we have no better proof than this that a convert need not immerse his utensils. This is not a case of a specific incident, rather this matter is relevant to every single convert who has ever converted. From the silence of the decisors of previous generations, we see that they did not require such. I have cited in many cases that which the Chazon Ish states (Shave'it Chapter 7, page 218) that in such cases that silence of the *poskim* is the "resolution superior to all other proofs."

Finally, Rabbi Weiss explains the substantive rule:

> As to the substance of the matter, it appears that the whole idea of immersing utensils is limited to cases where the utensil is transferred from owner to owner through a conveyance of title. When the utensil transfers from the title of the Gentile to the title of the Jew, that is when the duty to immerse applies . . . Such is not the case for a convert after conversion whose ownership of his utensils has not been abrogated and the utensil has not been transferred from one person to another. Thus there is no mitzva to immerse the utensils [of a newly converted person].

This approach inclines one to rule (as Rabbi Weiss notes) that it is better for a convert to immerse utensils without a *bracha*.

YD 121: *KASHERING* UTENSILS

A convert who observed *kashrut* before their conversion need not *kasher* one's utensils known to be kosher.[14] (When a utensil needs to be both immersed and *kashered*, the *kashering* is done first.[15])

YD 123: WINE OWNED FROM BEFORE CONVERSION

As a barrier against intermarriage, the Talmudic rabbis prohibited a Jew from drinking uncooked wine handled by a Gentile. However, a convert is permitted to drink any open bottles of wine that they touched prior to their conversion. Some authorities rule that others may not drink such wine due to the prohibition of *stam yeinam*. (See the similar debate in YD 113 above.) It makes most sense to permit

---

14. For more on this, see MHG p. 175.
15. YD 121:1; Pri Toar 121:4.

the wine for all[16] as long as the convert confirms that the wine was not used for pagan religious purposes.

YD 124: THE WINE OF A CONVERT WHO ABANDONS JUDAISM OUT OF FEAR

The wine of a convert who later abandons Judaism out of fear for their life is kosher[17] because most authorities rule that a convert who reverts to their prior faith out of fear is treated more leniently than a born-Jew who apostatizes out of fear. See OC 39 and YD 2 and CM 228.[18]

YD 146: IDOLATROUS RELIGIOUS OBJECTS THAT ARE INHERITED

As a general rule, a Jew is not allowed to own or even to receive any benefit or value from an item or food that was used in idolatrous worship. However, the sages allowed a convert whose parents died and left an inheritance that includes such items, to arrange with Gentile siblings to take these items in exchange for other items. Nonetheless, if a convert does take ownership of such items, one no longer may trade them with their siblings in exchange for other items; they must be destroyed.[19]

Laws of Loan Interest

YD 171: BORROWING OR LENDING WITH INTEREST

A Jew is not allowed to lend to, or borrow from, a fellow Jew with interest (absent a *heter iska*). This affects loans between converts and fellow Jews in the following ways:

---

16. Masechet Gerim 1:5; Rambam, Hilchot Mitamei Mishkav 10:7; MHG 176.
17. YD 119:9.
18. Cf. OC 39 and YD 119:9 and GvG 49. The counterargument is found in Aruch Hashulchan, OC 39:3 as regards such a convert writing *tefillin*.
19. Tur YD 146; Beit Yosef, YD 146:2; YD 146:4; CM 283:1.

A CONVERT CREDITOR COLLECTING INTEREST OWED AS A GENTILE

A Gentile who lent money to a Jew with interest, and later converted, may collect the interest if the Jew had provided them with some form of collateralized payment, such as a mortgage. If no collateral had been provided, some authorities still allow a convert to collect whatever interest was owed prior to conversion.[20] In any case, the convert definitely retains the rights to the principal of the loan – just as one retains the rights to damages for tort, breach of contract, or theft.[21]

A CONVERT DEBTOR PAYING INTEREST OWED AS A GENTILE

A convert who, as a Gentile, had borrowed money from a Jew with interest by means of a collateralized loan, is required to repay the interest. This is in order that people not claim that they converted to avoid paying the interest.[22] Others rule further that the convert must pay the interest even if the loan was not collateralized. Since the right to collect or even permission to pay the interest of a non-collateralized loan is disputed, the creditor should consider forgiving the convert's interest on such a loan.[23]

CHARGING INTEREST TO A NON-OBSERVANT CONVERT

Even if a convert stops practicing Judaism, a fellow Jew cannot charge

---

20. YD 171:1.

21. See Sefer Chasidim 691; Chazon Ish, Bava Kamma 10:14; Chavot Ya'ir 49.

22. YD 171:1.

23. Brit Yehuda 60:6–7. It is worth noting here that the Rosh (BM 5:57) permits this interest to be paid, even if such payment is indeed forbidden, in order to avoid besmirching the reputation of the convert. He notes that "Rava states: 'What is the reason for Rabbi Yossi's rule? So that people should not say that he converted for the money.' Therefore, he may make all interest payments even after he converted . . . even though it is a biblical prohibition to do so. The sages have the authority to uproot a Torah matter even when a transgression might be involved." (This might seem somewhat strange in light of the fact that elsewhere the Rosh follows the Tosafist tradition and makes it clear that the sages do not actually have the power to uproot Torah injunctions [Responsa Rosh 55:10]. However, perhaps the Tosafist tradition also states explicitly that even this view allows the rabbis to uproot a Torah injunction for sufficient cause (be-makom she-yesh panim ve-taam ba-davar). Thus, the Rosh might have understood that the biblical importance of loving a convert overrides the prohibition of paying or accepting interest.

them interest. This is because a non-observant convert is no different than any other non-observant Jew.[24]

Laws of *Nidda*

YD 183: NOT WAITING SEVEN DAYS BEFORE RESUMING MARITAL RELATIONS AFTER PRE-CONVERSION MENSTRUATION

Since Gentiles are not bound by the laws of menstruation, a *giyoret* who had menstruated before her conversion does not have to wait the required seven clean days before (remarrying[25] and) cohabitating with her husband.[26] However, a woman who converts while she is menstruating is rendered a *nidda* immediately upon her conversion.

YD 189: CALCULATING A MENSTRUAL CYCLE (A *VESET*)

A *giyoret* calculates her *veset* from her pre-conversion cycle. This is because menstrual cycles are based purely on biological phenomena.[27]

YD 192: DELAYING QUICK MARRIAGES ENTERED OUT OF DESIRE (*CHIMMUD*)

Although a couple must normally wait a minimum of seven days between an accepted proposal or a betrothal and the actual marriage due to concern about any excessive desire [on her part],[28] a converting married couple does not have to wait before marrying again in

---

24. Binyamin Zev 406.

25. The requirement to remarry is explained in EH 4.

26. Maharsham 3:204; Teshuvot Ravan 58; Igrot Moshe, EH 2:5; Shevet Halevi 10:233.

27. Maharsham 3:304. Based on a theological belief in a unique divine providence for Jews, however, Chazon Ish, YD 99:4 rules that for the first three months she must treat herself strictly as one who does not have a regular cycle until she has established as a Jewess how God relates nature to her cycle.

28. These days of delaying marriages that might otherwise be entered hastily out of desire (*mishum chimmud*) are also sometimes described as days of waiting after the woman might have experienced highly rare bleeding in anticipation of intimacy (*dam chimud*).

accordance with halacha. This is because there is no concern about excessive desire.[29]

Laws of Vows

YD 203: PRE-CONVERSION VOWS

Since the prohibition against violating one's vows does not apply to Gentiles, a convert is not bound by any vows of renunciation made prior to conversion.[30] There is some discussion, however, on the question of whether a convert who had made a vow of performance as a Gentile is obligated to fulfill the oath as a Jew.[31]

YD 217: THE TERM "JEWS" IN VOWS INCLUDES CONVERTS

One who makes a vow not to receive benefit from a Jew (*yisrael*) or even from the progeny of Abraham (*zera Avraham*) may not derive benefit from a convert either.[32] A convert is a full-fledged Jew and a spiritual descendant of Abraham and Sarah, as mentioned above in entry OC 53.

YD 234: THE RIGHTS OF A CONVERT FATHER TO CANCEL A YOUNG CONVERT DAUGHTER'S VOW

If a man and his daughter convert, it is unclear whether he is viewed as her father who can cancel her early adolescent vows.[33] The better answer, however, is that he is not allowed to cancel her vows.[34]

---

29. Igrot Moshe, YD 1:86.

30. Beit Yitzchak, OC 92 (at the end); Mishne L'melech, Hilchot Melachim 10:7; MHG. 174.

31. Beit Yitzchak, OC 92, rules that the convert is not obligated to fulfill the oath. The opinion that the convert is obligated to fulfill it appears more persuasive.

32. Tur, YD 217; YD 217:40, 43.

33. Or can collect her betrothal money if he grants her hand in betrothal when she is still a prepubescent girl or beginning early adolescence, or can collect (on behalf of his daughter) special additional fined monies that a rapist could often owe a father if he rapes a young virgin girl.

34. Shut Levushei Mordechai EH first edition no. 38, Shut Beit Yitzchak EH 1:29:4.

Laws of Honoring One's Parents and the Elderly

YD 240: HONORING ONE'S BIOLOGICAL PARENTS

There is a debate whether a convert, as a newborn person, is subject to the *mitzva* of honoring their biological parents (Gentile or Jewish[35]).[36] In any case, it is clear that a convert is forbidden to hit, denigrate, or curse their parents, and must honor them to some degree as a measure of gratitude for raising them,[37] lest the convert allow themselves to drop in holiness or sensitivity.[38] For example: some *poskim* state that a convert should pray for the health/recovery of Gentile parents and should continue to visit and interact with non-Jewish parents, as long as such interaction does not compromise halacha or negatively influence the convert's Jewish children.[39] In parallel, a convert should extend all the courtesies and gestures of respect that are common in the secular world to their Gentile parents.[40]

YD 240: A BORN-JEW MARRYING A CONVERT IN SPITE OF PARENTS' WISHES

Someone whose parents object to their marriage choice is permitted to ignore them to marry a convert.[41]

YD 244: STANDING FOR AN ELDERLY CONVERT

Although a convert is considered newborn in terms of identity (*ger shenitgayer k'tinok she'nolad dami*), one must stand for an elderly con-

---

35. The issue is the same in both scenarios because the convert is considered newborn (OPG 190).

36. Yad Eliyahu 40; Igrot Moshe, YD 2:130; Aseh Lecha Rav 6:62; Teshuvot V'hanhagot 2:507.

37. Rambam, Hilchot Mamrim 5:11.

38. Rambam, Hilchot Mamrim 5:11; Tur, YD 241; Perisha, YD 241:14; YD 241:9; Levush 241:9; Aruch Hashulchan, YD 241:10–11.

39. OPG 159.

40. For example, in my view, it is a proper policy for American converts to send parents Mother's Day and Father's Day cards.

41. Kanei Bosn 2:91. GvG 50.

vert just as one must stand for any elderly person out of respect for
their age, even if the elderly person only recently converted.[42]

Laws of Charity

YD 248: IS A MINOR CONVERT CONSIDERED PARENTLESS SO AS TO RECEIVE CHARITY?

Although a convert is considered newborn in terms of identity (*ger shenitgayer k'tinok she'nolad dami*), a minor convert whose biological father and mother support them is not viewed as a poor waif entitled to community charity funds. Although some disagree, lest the father pressure the son to renege on Judaism,[43] there is little reason to disagree when state law compels such support.

YD 251: PROVIDING CHARITY TO ONE'S GENTILE RELATIVES

It appears that a convert, as a newborn, does not have any formal *tzedaka* obligations towards Gentile relatives. See above entry YD 248. Nevertheless, according to the laws of peaceful living, such *tzedaka* should be extended.

A CONVERT'S RIGHT TO CHARITY

Some say that a convert takes priority over a born-Jew in the allocation of charity funds because, on top of the obligation to help one's fellow, there is an obligation to love the convert.[44] Others prioritize the born-Jew as someone who – whether as an individual or as part of an historically Jewish family – has had an earlier right.[45] Although the weight of the precedent is in favor of prioritizing the born-Jew, there is logic to the alternative as well. A fine compromise might be to have no set priority at all, which would manifest love of the convert.

---

42. Yad Shaul, YD 244. KhG 53 at page 120.
43. Tzitz Eliezer 18:73:7.
44. Pri Megadim, OC 156, EA 2.
45. YD 251:9.

Laws of Circumcision of Sons

YD 260: CIRCUMCISION OF A SON CONCEIVED BEFORE CONVERSION

One who converts and receives a newborn identity while his wife is pregnant is not technically obligated to circumcise his biological son born from this pregnancy.[46] This means, for example, that he need not formally appoint the *mohel* as his agent for the circumcision. See entry CM 283.

Laws of Conversion

YD 268: ADOPTING A JEWISH NAME

When a person converts to Judaism, the convert should adopt a Hebrew name.[47] Although there was a time when converts adopted the Hebrew names of Abraham and Sarah exclusively, that is no longer the case. Converts do adopt the patriarch Abraham and matriarch Sarah as their parents. See OC 139 and EH 129.

BLESSING *SHEHECHEYANU* FOLLOWING CONVERSION

There is a dispute between Ashkenazi and Sephardic authorities as to whether a convert should bless God upon converting. According to Ashkenazi tradition, the convert does not bless *shehecheyanu*, while according to Sephardic authorities the convert does bless *shehecheyanu* immediately after emerging from the *mikva*.[48] The Sephardic Radvaz[49] argues that inasmuch as one blesses *shehecheyanu* the first time they perform certain mitzvot, one should definitely bless *shehecheyanu* the first time one is obligated in all the mitzvot! The Nahar

---

46. Divrei Yetziv, YD 2:167; Mishne Halachot 17:32.

47. This is the near-universal practice in the Jewish community (KhG 38 at p.93). There is no firm halachic source for this custom, and it is worth noting that Ruth did not change her name (ibid, n. 38).

48. Radvaz 434; Birkei Yosef, YD 268:3; Minchat Yitzchak 1:129; Mishne Halachot 16:94.

49. Radvaz 1:434, cited in Pitchei Teshuva, YD 268:1.

Mitzrayim[50] notes that the customary way to address this dispute is for the convert to wear a new garment and to bless God for this event with the new garment.[51] Different rabbinical courts have different customs, and each should follow its own practice.[52]

A CONVERT WHO APOSTATIZES

A convert who abandons Judaism or reverts back to his original religion (after a valid conversion) is considered a sinful Jew, but does not revert to being a Gentile.[53] Rather, the convert is considered to be a Jewish apostate whose wine, bread, and slaughtering of meat are forbidden and who does not count towards a prayer quorum.[54] If a convert abandoned Judaism out of fear for their life (such as in a Crusade attack), the convert is not even considered a sinful Jew.[55]

A CONVERT SERVING ON A RABBINICAL COURT OF CONVERSION

There is much discussion regarding whether one can convert via a *bet din* that includes a convert. Some authorities accept such conversions without qualms; some authorities merely validate them *de facto*; some authorities view them as invalid.[56] Therefore, it is best that a convert not serve on a *bet din* of conversion so that the three rabbis not violate the mitzva to love the new convert by effecting a conversion that will be called into question. Nonetheless, most authorities rule that such conversion need not be repeated.[57]

---

50. Nahar Mitzrayim, Gerut 21.
51. See Minchat Yitzchak 1:129.
52. Rabbi Steven Chaim Lindenblatt, in a email communication with this author, notes that Rabbi Moshe Feinstein instructed converts to bless *shehecheyanu*.
53. See for example, Yevamot 47b; Bechorot 30b; Rambam, Hilchot Isurei Biah 13:13; YD 268:2; Taz YD 268:16; and Aruch Hashulchan, YD 268:8.
54. Aruch Hashulchan, OC 39:3 and other locations.
55. Therefore his slaughter is valid, he may write a Torah, and his wine is considered kosher. See YD 119:9.
56. See for example (in no particular order), *Bet Mordechai* 1:80, *Piskei Din Yerushalayim Dinai Mamonut uBerurai Yahadut* 5:40 and 7:107, *Maaneh Eliyahu* 88, *Lev Aryeh* 88, *Sheerit Yisrael* YD 22, *Chukat Hager* 6:10, *Luach Yerushalayim* 10 (5710), *Tzitz Eliezer* 13:80, *Tiferet Tzvi* 1:72, *Nachalat Tzvi* 1:226, *Shalmei Shmuel* 45, *Bemareh Habazak* 3:82, *Mishnat Hager* 3:19, *Minchat Shlomo* 225, Rabbi SY Elyashiv *Hearot LaMesechet Kidushin* 436, *Otzar Piskei Gerim* 47 (page 207), *Halichot Shlomo* YD 268:3, and Rabbi Hershel Schachter, *Kol Tzvi* 5762 (299–301).
57. See my essay "May a Convert be a Member of a Rabbinical Court for

Laws of Sacred Writings

YD 281: WRITING A TORAH, *TEFILLIN* OR *MEZUZA*

Although some authorities rule that a convert cannot write a valid Torah scroll due to the fact that some commandments do not apply to him, the accepted view is that he can write Torah scrolls,[58] *tefillin*, and *mezuzot*.[59]

YD 285: AFFIXING A *MEZUZA* ANEW AFTER CONVERSION

As a Jew newly obligated to affix *mezuza* scrolls on their doorposts, a convert should promptly re-affix any *mezuzot* that were placed prior to the conversion. Even the position that has a tenant renting outside of Israel wait thirty days would obligate a convert to affix (or re-affix) a *mezuza* immediately in a residence in which the convert has been living for thirty days.[60]

Laws of Agrarian Living

YD 296: THE INJUNCTION AGAINST *KILAYIM*

A convert's pre-conversion mixtures of seeds and species (*kilayim*) may be used freely by the convert or any other Jew if they were planted by the Gentile in their own field without any help from a Jew; Gentiles, according to most authorities, are not obligated in that commandment. This is exactly like a Jew deriving benefit from the *kilayim* of a Gentile, which is permissible as long as no Jew, or their property, is involved.[61]

Conversion," *Journal of Halacha and Contemporary Society* 59 (2010): 61–78 and my posting at http://www.torahmusings.com/2012/07/convert-on-a-bet-din-for -conversion/, and the relevant supplemental essay in this book.

58. YD 281:2; Shach, YD 281:6 (slaves); Mishbetzot Zahav, OC 691:2, Eishel Avraham, OC 39:9; Tzitz Eliezer 14:19.

59. OC 39:3; Eishel Avraham, OC 39:9; Tzitz Eliezer 14:19.

60. Agur B'ohalecha page 366:36. Similarly, a convert who had tied their own *tzitzit* before conversion, must retie them.

61. YD 297:2 and commentaries. Others rule that a Gentile is obligated in this

YD 305: A CONVERT WHO IS A FIRSTBORN FROM HIS GENTILE MOTHER

The obligation of redeeming a firstborn son (*pidyon haben*) does not apply to a firstborn convert inasmuch as he was not born as the *peter rechem* (first out of the womb) of a Jewish mother.[62]

THE FIRST JEWISH CHILD BORN TO A CONVERT WHO HAS HAD CHILDREN PRIOR TO CONVERSION

Although a convert has the status of a new person in some ways, the first Jewish child born to a *giyoret* who has had children previously is not considered the first of her womb – such a son is not redeemed as a firstborn.[63]

YD 318: FIRSTBORN ANIMALS

A convert must give firstborn kosher animals of their flock to a Kohen only if they were born after the conversion. If there is some doubt as to when the animal was born, it should be left to become blemished somehow and may then be kept by the convert.[64]

YD 330: SEPARATING A PORTION FROM DOUGH (*CHALLA*) AFTER CONVERSION

Only dough kneaded after conversion is subject to the mitzva of separating a portion (*challa*).[65] If someone else kneaded the convert's dough and it is unclear whether it was kneaded before or after the conversion, the convert should separate *challa* without a blessing.[66]

YD 331: *SHEMITTA* PRODUCE HARVESTED BEFORE CONVERSION

The Torah calls for an agricultural Sabbatical year. A Jew's produce in Israel can be forbidden if not shared, and it is limited in its permitted

---

commandment, although it is not clear how this may be applied in the case of a convert.
  62. YD 305:20–21.
  63. Levush, YD 305:21.
  64. Chullin 134b; YD 318:5.
  65. YD 330:4.
  66. Challa 3:6; Rashi, Chullin 134a; Teshuvot Harashba 1:54; YD 330:4; Shach, YD 330:8 (no blessing); Taz, YD 330:3; Vayan Yosef, YD 19.

uses.[67] However, a farmer convert's pre-conversion *shemitta* produce is permitted without limitations. This is because normative halacha follows the view that a non-Jew's produce is not subject to the laws of *shemitta*.[68]

FIRST FRUITS *(BIKKURIM)*

In line with the rulings that converts are fully associated with *klal Yisrael* and pray in the language of collective Israel, most authorities agree that a farmer convert offering their first fruits in Temple times even thanks God for the land that He "swore to our ancestors to give us."[69]

YD 332: LEAVING FALLEN GLEANINGS, FORGOTTEN SHEAVES, AND A PORTION OF THE FIELD AND ORCHARD FOR THE POOR

A farmer in the land of Israel who converts after the harvest is not obligated to leave *leket*, *shikhecha*, and *pe'ah* for the poor.[70]

Laws of Mourning

YD 374: MOURNING FOR ONE'S CONVERSION RABBI

Some authorities maintain that a convert must tear their clothes *(keria)* upon hearing of the death of the rabbi who converted them, as anyone would do for their rabbinic mentor *(rebbi muvhak)*.[71]

---

67. The laws of *shemitta* produce are too complex to discuss in this work of unique laws for converts.

68. See Avkat Rochel 22–25 and Mabit 1:11, 21, 217, 396.

69. Rambam, Hilchot Bikkurim 4:3; Biur Hagra, OC 139:3; Birkei Yosef, OC 199:1; Teshuvot Harashba 7:54; Teshuvot Radvaz 5:220; Shvut Yaakov 3:15; Igrot Moshe, OC 2:113; Sefer Haroke'ach, Hilchot Seudah 331. This rule, which is really limited to Temple times, is cited here because it is foundational to many other rules.

70. Mishna Peah 4:6; Rambam, Matnot Aniyim 2:9, Shut Ri Migash no. 7; MHG 172.

71. Sha'ar Ephraim 91; Pitchei Teshuva, YD 242:15.

Common custom, however, is not in accordance with this view – unless the rabbi was indeed one's *rebbi muvhak*.

MOURNING FOR A CONVERT'S FAMILY MEMBERS

Because all the familial connections of a convert are severed upon being newly born (see entry YD 248), there is no absolute obligation for a family who converts together to mourn one another's passing.[72] The custom, however, is that they do mourn such deaths and that members of the community express condolences for the loss.[73]

PROPRIETY OF MOURNING FOR GENTILE RELATIVES

It is proper and healthy for a convert to mourn the passing of members of his immediate biological family. Thus, a *ger* may lead a quorum in prayers to mark their mourning. The convert may also choose to sanctify God with *kaddish*,[74] since the *kaddish* sanctification is a way of praying for the souls of the deceased, and in all the other ways typical of Jewish mourning that they so choose, as long as they do not conflict with fulfilling obligated mitzvot.[75] However, the convert does not have the status of a relative who is exempt from mitzvot prior to the funeral (an *onen*). Nor is a *ger* exempt from wearing *tefillin* on the day of the death and burial.[76]

---

72. Tur YD 374, Beit Yosef YD 374:5, YD 374:5; Teshuvot V'hanhagot 1:684. See also KhG 60 at page 127.

73. I have been told that some have the practice to actually sit *shiva* fully. Although I have not seen this noted anywhere, it is certainly permitted to do so. Such is noted in Rabbi Maurice Lamm's work, *Becoming a Jew (Middle Village, NY: Jonathan David, 1991), pp. 249–250*.

74. See also entry OC 116. As the recently deceased eminent scholar Rabbi Maurice Lamm, noted in his work, *Darka Shel HaYahadut BeMavet Uve'Aveilut* (p. 210), it is proper as a general matter for a convert to mourn for his biological parents.

75. Yechaveh Da'at 6:60; Teshuvot V'hanhagot 2:43; Yalkut Yosef OC 56:32, YD 30:25.

76. KhG 61 at page 127.

Even Haezer

Procreation • Permitted and Forbidden Marriage Partners •
Celebrating Weddings • Marital Obligations and Rights • Divorce •
Levirate Marriage and Release • Raped or Seduced Child

Laws of Procreation

EH 1: PROCREATION

The children that a convert had before he converted fulfill his obligation to procreate (*pru u'rvu*) because a convert need not be halachically related to his children to be credited with having procreated.
Although some authorities rule that this is only true if the children
convert so that he retroactively procreated more Jews,[1] most authorities rule that a convert fulfilled this obligation even if his children
remain non-Jewish since the obligation is to procreate humanity.[2]

Laws of Permitted and Forbidden
Marriage Partners

EH 2: PROVING THAT ONE IS JEWISH AND A VALID MARRIAGE PARTNER

All Jews are sometimes required to prove that they are Jewish and eligible to marry a potential spouse.[3] This applies equally to a convert.[4]

---

1. Yevamot 62b; Rambam, Hilchot Ishut 15:6; EH 1:7; Levush, EH 1:7; Beit
Shmuel, EH 1:12; Chelkat Mechokek, EH 1:9; Radvaz 7:2; Tzitz Eliezer 4:16:10;
Aruch Hashulchan, EH 1:19; Pri Yitzchak 2:60; Maharil 196.
2. Aruch Hashulchan, EH 1:19.
3. Beit Shmuel, EH 2:3.
4. For a discussion of how marriage between a Jew and a questionable convert
is a serious issue (*davar sh'be'erva*) and when proof is needed, see Igrot Moshe,

EH 4: IT IS COMMENDABLE TO MARRY A CONVERT

The Talmud teaches that it is commendable to marry a convert.[5]

PERMITTED MARRIAGES BETWEEN CONVERTS AND FELLOW JEWS

A convert and a Levite, Israelite, fellow convert, *petzua daka* (a man who is anatomically sterile or reproductively injured),[6] or the daughter of a Kohen[7] may marry each other. Although a convert and a *mamzer* may also marry each other, such marriage should be discouraged since the child of such a marriage is a *mamzer*.[8]

MARRIAGE BETWEEN AN EDOMITE OR AMMONITE CONVERT AND A BORN-JEW

Although according to Torah law a born Jew/ess and an Edomite man or woman convert or an Ammonite or Moabite man convert may not marry each other, no restrictions apply to any race or nation today because these Biblical era nations have disappeared.[9]

MARRIAGE BETWEEN AN EGYPTIAN CONVERT AND A BORN-JEW

Admittedly, the Rosh rules to continue applying the Biblical restrictions to modern-day Egyptians, but the Rambam and normative halacha rule that modern-day Egyptians are no longer Biblical era Egyptians.[10]

EH 6: A CONVERT MARRYING A KOHEN'S DAUGHTER

A Kohen may not marry a *giyoret*.[11]

YD 2:127.

5. Horayot 13a. See also Sefer Chasidim 377. But see Mishne Halachot 9:237.
6. Shulchan Aruch 4:23.
7. See EH 7.
8. Beit Yosef, EH 4:22; EH 4:22.
9. Rambam, Hilchot Issurei Biah, 12:25; EH 4:9.
10. Rambam Isurai Biah 12:25, EH 4:10. See also Otzar Haposkim 4:10, 27; Birkei Yosef, EH 4:1 and many others. And see previous law.
11. Either because a Kohen must marry a born Jewess, or because a *giyoret* is classified as a *zona*, or because the term *zona* sometimes means one not born of a Jewish mother. Shulchan Aruch EH 6:8 and comments of both Chelkat

Although a true Kohen[12] and a *giyoret* are forbidden to marry each other[13] (unless he is a *petzua daka*[14] – above EH 4), a *ger* and the daughter of a true Kohen may marry each other.[15]

THE DAUGHTER OF CONVERTS MARRYING A KOHEN

There is a debate over the permissibility of a Kohen and a daughter of two converts marrying each other. If they did so, they are not forced to divorce.[16]

BEING INTIMATE WITH AN APOSTATE CONVERT DOES NOT INVALIDATE A WOMAN IN MARRIAGE TO A KOHEN

Since an apostate convert remains a Jew, a Jewish woman who has been intimate with such an apostate may marry a Kohen.[17]

EH 9: A *GIYORET* WHOSE TWO PREVIOUS HUSBANDS DIED

A *giyoret* who lost two husbands prior to her conversion is viewed the same as any other Jewish woman whose two previous husbands died; if their deaths can be attributed to specific causes unrelated to her, she is not categorized as dangerous (*katlanit*).[18] In any case, common custom is to be as lenient as possible on this issue. [19]

Mechokek 6:9 and Bet Shmuel 6:15.

12. Rabbi Feinstein notes that sometimes people think that they are Kohanim when they really are not (Igrot Moshe EH 4:11 and 4:39).

13. Rambam, Hilchot Issurei Biah 18:1–3; EH 6:1, 8; Igrot Moshe, EH 1:11.

14. Ritva Yevamot 60b; Rambam, Hilchot Issurei Biah 16:1; EH 5:1; Igrot Moshe, EH 1:11.

According to many *poskim*, they may remain married should the man later recover. (The Beit Yitzchak 35 discusses this, and the Shulchan Shlomo, Refuah 3:69 rules this way.)

15. EH 7:22.

16. See Shulchan Aruch EH 7:21. For more on this, see "Who is a Ger" at http://www.torahmusings.com/2012/11/who-is-a-ger/. And see the related supplemental essay at the end of this book.

17. Mishpatai Uziel Tinyana 2:56 rules otherwise, but is rejected by Yabia Omer YD 1:11:5 and KhG 34 page 87–88 in line with the halachic consensus that an apostate convert is still Jewish.

18. Amudei Or 81.

19. See Otzar Haposkim EH 9.

EH 10: REMARRYING ONE'S FORMERLY GENTILE EX-SPOUSE WHO HAD MARRIED ANOTHER IN THE INTERIM

Two converts who had divorced each other before conversion and had since married others may, nonetheless, remarry each other. This is because the marriage and divorce done as Gentiles bear no halachic significance after conversion.[20]

EH 13: A MARRIED NEW *GIYORET* AND THE LAW OF WAITING NINETY DAYS BEFORE REMARRYING

Although the Shulchan Aruch rules that a *giyoret* must wait ninety days after her conversion before remarrying, in order to determine whether any child she might be carrying was conceived before or after conversion, many authorities rule that no wait is required when it is clear whether she is or is not pregnant.[21] If she is obviously pregnant, menstruating, post-menopausal, or otherwise clearly not pregnant, such a delay is unnecessary.[22]

However, like any other pregnant or nursing Jewish woman, a pregnant or nursing convert is normally forbidden to marry anybody other than the child's father for eighteen to twenty-four months after birth.[23]

A PREGNANT OR NURSING CONVERT AND THE CHILD'S BIOLOGICAL FATHER MAY MARRY EACH OTHER

Although conversion severs the halachic connection between child and father, there is no prohibition on a pregnant or nursing *giyoret*

---

20. Maharam Chalava 5; Chelkat Ya'akov, EH 34:2. But see also Ran to Sanhedrin 58b.

21. Tur, EH 13; Beit Yosef, YD 269:9; Bach, EH 13:3; YD 269:9; EH 13:5, Levush, EH 13:5; Mishne L'melech, Hilchot Gerushin 11:21; Teshuvot V'hanhagot 3:303; Dagul M'revava, EH 13:5; Chelkat Mechokek, EH 13:4; Pirchei Kehuna, EH 11; Aruch Hashulchan, EH 13:6; Igrot Moshe, EH 2:5; Yabia Omer 9:17, Mishne Halachot 17:20; OPG 175.

22. Mishne L'melech, Hilchot Gerushin 11:21; Dagul M'revava, EH 13:5; Chelkat Mechokek, EH 13:4; Pirchei Kehuna, EH 11; Igrot Moshe, EH 2:5; Yabia Omer 9:17, Mishne Halachot 17:20. OPG 175.

23. Although conversion severs the halachic familial connection between the fetus or child and the father, the explicit point of this decree is to protect a child from dying from neglect under a man other than the biological father (*meuberet chaveiro/meineket chaveiro*). See Otzar Haposkim 13:72 (5).

marrying a *ger* who is the biological father of the child. This is because, as the biological father of the child, it is presumed that the *ger*, like all fathers, will take care of his child.[24]

EH 15: RELATIVES WHOM A CONVERT MAY NOT MARRY

Since a convert is considered newly born through conversion, basic (Biblical) law allows a convert to marry biological relatives. Nevertheless, the Talmud Sages decreed that a convert is forbidden to marry relatives lest they experience or appear to experience a drop in holiness.[25] Some authorities rule that this applies only to relatives that the Torah forbids to Gentiles; maternal siblings are forbidden to marry each other and a maternal sister is forbidden to marry her sister's ex-husband as long as the divorced sister is still alive.[26] However, others forbid marriage both between paternal relatives and between relatives for whom local Gentile culture considers marriage to be sinful[27] – and possibly even between those with whom Jews forbid marriage, as an extra stringency.[28]

MARRIAGE BETWEEN ONE MAN AND MOTHER AND DAUGHTER CONVERTS

A man may not marry a *giyoret* and her converted daughter or mother so long as the original *giyoret* is alive.[29]

BROTHERS MARRYING EACH OTHER'S WIVES

According to rabbinic law, the prohibition against marrying one's brother's wife applies to brothers who convert. Although the law as regards paternal, but not maternal, brothers is disputed, common custom is to rule stringently.[30]

---

24. The view taken by Even Yekara (1:11) that a nursing convert cannot marry the father of the child until after the child is weaned is not normative.

25. B. Yevamot 22a.

26. Rambam Issurei Bi'ah 14:12–13; YD 269:5–7.

27. Tosafot to Yevamot 22a; Ritva to Yevamot 22a; Aruch Hashulchan, YD 269:6–7; Tzitz Eliezer 17:49.

28. Noda B'Yehuda, Mahadura Kama, EH 26 versus Teshuvot Rabbi Akiva Eiger, Mahadura Tinyana, 68.

29. YD 269:5–6.

30. Rambam, Hilchot Issurei Biah 14:15; Tur, YD 269; YD 269:3; Levush, EH 157:3; Aruch Hashulchan, YD 269:2–3.

MARRIAGE BETWEEN A MAN AND TWO CONVERTED SISTERS

One could theoretically argue that a man and the paternal biological sister of his divorced *giyoret* ex-wife may marry each other even according to the strict view. That is because the man and the second woman are not paternal or maternal relatives, the two sisters are merely paternally related, and secular American society does not deem marrying two sisters sequentially as inappropriate. However, it seems reasonable that the authorities who forbid both marriage between paternal relatives and marriage between relatives whom Gentile society forbids to each other, actually forbid any marriage that is forbidden between Jews.

EH 11: MARRIAGE BETWEEN A CONVERT AND A JEW/ESS WHO HAD A SEXUAL RELATIONSHIP WHEN THE CONVERT WAS A GENTILE

In spite of an ongoing halachic debate,[31] custom allows a Jewish man and a Gentile woman in a relationship – and especially in a civil marriage – to remarry after her conversion. This includes a case where the Gentile woman was married to another man at the time of the initial sexual relationship.[32]

A Jewish man and a married Jewish woman who had an affair may never marry each other.[33] Normative halacha, however, after much debate, allows marriage between a *ger* and a formerly married Jewish woman with whom he had an affair when he was a Gentile.[34] It follows, therefore, that a *ger* and a single Jewish woman with whom he had a sexual relationship before his conversion certainly may marry.[35]

EH 18: A PERSON WHO WAS MARRIED AS A GENTILE IS HALACHICALLY SINGLE UPON CONVERSION

A convert is not halachically married to a pre-conversion spouse.

---

31. Yevamot 24b with Rashi; Ramban, Hilchot Yevamot 24b; EH 11:5. See also Igrot Moshe, EH 1:27.

32. As there is no prohibition.

33. *Asurah echad l'baal echad l'bo'el.*

34. Rosh Ketubot 1:4; Beit Yosef, EH 178:19; EH 178:19; Chaim Shaul 1:49; MHG. 136; KhG 9. Page 25. Although there is a slight contradiction between EH 11:6 and EH 178:19, common custom is to be lenient.

35. Or Same'ach 32; MHG, pp. 133–136.

Even if a couple converted together, each of them is single[36] until they remarry.[37]

EH 20: THE GENDER OF A CONVERT WHO HAD UNDERGONE SEX REASSIGNMENT SURGERY

The gender of a convert who had undergone sex reassignment surgery before conversion is debated. This might or might not be related to the question of whether gender reassignment surgery is in general effective as a matter of Jewish law.[38]

EH 22: THE ISSUE OF *YICHUD* (SECLUSION) WITH FAMILY MEMBERS OF THE OPPOSITE GENDER

Although a convert is viewed as born anew (*ke'tinok she'nolad dami*) and previous familial relations are severed in most ways, a convert may be secluded with immediate relatives of the opposite gender – whether Jewish or Gentile – in all the ways halacha permits seclusion between different family members.[39] (It follows, therefore, that a Jewish man may be alone with his Gentile daughter.[40])

EH 26: A COUPLE REMARRIES AFTER CONVERSION

A couple that converts together and wishes to remain married must marry in accordance with Jewish law – with a *chuppa* and with *kiddu-shin*.[41]

---

36. Rema, YD 269:9.

37. See entry EH 26. However, if the couple publicly continues to live together as married even without a ceremony, they might be considered married.

38. See Rabbi Eden Ben Efraim, Dor Tahapuchot (Jerusalem, 5764) pages 73–74 for a discussion of the unique matter of conversion, and see that work throughout for a discussion of gender assignment in general.

39. Igrot Moshe, EH 4:64; Mishne Halachot 17:31; Teshuvot V'hanhagot 1:776; L'horot Natan 7:87. But see B'tzel Hachochma (4:14) who forbids being completely secluded (*yichud mi-deorraita*).

40. GvG 57.

41. Darchei Moshe, YD 269:3; YD 269:9.

Laws of Celebrating Weddings

EH 62: *SHEVA BRACHOT* FOR A CONVERTING COUPLE THAT REMARRIES

A married couple (or possibly even one that is functionally married[42]) that converts and remarries observes just one day of festive blessings (*sheva berachot*) – similar both to a couple that remarries after divorcing and to a married couple that becomes observant (*ba'alei teshuva*) and undergoes a halachic marriage ceremony.[43] This is because seven days of celebratory *sheva berachot* are generally observed only if one of the parties was never married, while this couple had been married as Gentiles.[44] There is a minority opinion that a formerly intermarried couple that remarries after the Gentile partner converts should celebrate with *sheva berachot* for seven days inasmuch as marriage between a Jew and a Gentile is not recognized halachically.[45]

Laws of Marital Obligations and Rights

EH 66–67: WORDING OF *KETUBAH* FOR A *GER* OR A *GIYORET*

In writing a *ketubah*:
1. The custom is that a *ger's* or *giyoret's* name is written "[Hebrew name[46]] son/daughter of the patriarch Avraham" (\בֶן פלונית

---

42. Such as when they lived together for many years without marriage but acted as if they were married and had children together.

43. Shevet Halevi 4:173; Chaim Shaul 2:38; MHG 136.

44. OPG 181 quotes views that permit the two converts who marry to celebrate with blessings for seven days. The argument supporting that view is that we generally adopt the view of Chatam Sofer that a couple that slept together before marriage (sinfully) nonetheless celebrates with *sheva brachot* whenever it is a first marriage for both of them. Thus, this couple should do the same since, as newborn converts, this is considered the first marriage, although they obviously slept together beforehand. The counter-argument is that Chatam Sofer discussed the joy of marrying for the first time that people feel even if the couple had been having sex without marriage, but this couple had been married as Gentiles.

45. OPG 182, who cites no sources for his position.

46. A convert's Hebrew name is written even if the name is not expected to be widely used (normative practice for good reason [*de facto*]). Nonetheless, a

בת אברהם אבינו or פלונית בן\בת אאע"ה). However, some leading authorities rule that a convert who was raised Jewish is called the son/daughter of the Jewish adoptive or biological convert father as long as a *giyoret* notes that she is a convert.[47] A convert is entitled to adopt the approach that he or she prefers as long as some mention of her convert status is made.

2. As regards the designation every bride must be given, a *giyoret* is described only as a "convert" (גיורתא).[48] If there is some familial tension over assigning her a convert designation,[49] the word "woman" (איתתא) can be used.[50]

3. A virgin *giyoret* bride's minimal *ketubah* sum is the standard 200 *zuz* (מאתים ... מדאורייתא)[51] even if she had converted after toddlerhood,[52] and a non-virgin *giyoret* bride's minimal *ketubah* sum is the standard 100 *zuz* (מאה ... מדרבנן) [53] – even if she is remarrying her husband whom she had originally married as a virgin.[54]

---

ketubah written with a convert's Gentile name is valid *de facto* (EH 129:6, Taz, EH 129:7; Beit Shmuel, EH 129:39; Teshuvot Harosh 17:11; Tzitz Eliezer 21:1; Avnei Ha'ephod 17; Mishne Halachot 4:171).

47. Minchat Yitzchak 1:136; Yalkut Yosef, EH 5:4; Sova Smachot 1:5:4.

48. Radvaz as cited in Pitchei Teshuva, EH 67:1. But see Haketubah Kehilchata 11:28 who notes that it is ideally proper as regards a divorcee after conversion to mention both.

49. For example: she converted after her mother's doubtfully valid or invalid conversion but she or other family members consider the mother Jewish from birth.

50. This is based on the practice to write the word איתתא ("woman") in any situation where the woman may not marry a Kohen (Teshuvot Vehanhagot 1:759; Shevet Levi 8:285; Piskei Din [Jerusalem] Financial Matters and Lineage 7:445; and Rav Moshe Feinstein according to reports this writer has received).

A ketubah of a convert which makes no allusion to the fact that the person is a convert – neither in their name nor in any other manner – ought to be rewritten to reflect their status as a convert (for reasons explained well in Bemareh Habazak 7:98 at page 294).

51. Rambam, Hilchot Ishut 11:2–3; EH 67:3.

52. See views collected in Otzar Haposkim 67:3:2). (Many disagree even if she definitely is a virgin [noted in ibid] and write instead מאה ... מדרבנן). But logic inclines one to accept that an observant convert who testifies about her status ought to be believed and then assumes that status. Out of love of the convert, this view is here adopted as normative.

53. Rambam, Hilchot Ishut 11:2–3; EH 67:3.

54. Ketubot 90a; Darchei Moshe, EH 100:21; EH 67:11; Igrot Moshe, EH 1:101; Yad Eliyahu 40.

READING THE *KETUBAH* OUT LOUD

It is worth noting that there is no Jewish law obligation to read the exact text of the *ketubah* out loud at a wedding, and a convert can choose whether or not one wishes to have their status read aloud.[55]

EH 67: PRE-CONVERSION FINANCIAL AGREEMENTS BETWEEN SPOUSES

All pre-conversion financial agreements between spouses remain valid and enforceable – even if they choose not to remarry.[56]

EH 75: THE RIGHT TO MOVE TO ISRAEL AGAINST A SPOUSE'S WISHES

As a Jew, a convert is obligated in the mitzva of settling in the land of Israel (*yishuv ha'aretz*).[57] Thus, just as any spouse who wishes to move to Israel is halachically considered in the right, so too a convert spouse.

Laws of Divorce

EH 129: PARENTAL IDENTIFICATION IN A *GET*

Common custom is that the name of a *ger* or *giyoret* in a divorce *get* is written as "[Hebrew name and secular names] son/daughter of the patriarch Abraham" (פלונית ... בן\בת אברהם אבינו or ... פלוני בן\בת אאע"ה).[58] Although there is some discussion whether a man or woman who converted along with their father uses the father's Jewish name,[59] it seems from the Shulchan Aruch that the preferred approach is to write *ben Avraham Avinu*.

A *get* written with a convert's Gentile name alone because the Hebrew name was never truly used, or in which an old unused

---

55. As many have recounted, and as I have seen countless times.
56. Ketubot 90b; MHG 184.
57. Furthermore: If even a slave is obligated and has the right to move to the Land of Israel (YD 267), then a convert certainly is obligated and has the right (MHG 172).
58. Beit Yosef, EH 129:20; Darchei Moshe, EH 129:27; EH 129:6,9,20; Teshuvot Harashba 1:556; Teshuvot Harosh; Radvaz 1:376.
59. Mishpetei Uziel, YD 2:59.

Gentile name was added as one of the convert's current names, is valid *de facto.*[60]

THE SEPHARDIC TEXT OF A *GET*

In a *get* that is written in accordance with the Sephardic tradition, reference is made to the possibility of the husband's or wife's father having additional names (ולאבהתי) in case some people know the party as the son and daughter of such named man. Since this concern does not apply to a convert son or daughter of the patriarchal father Abraham, most Sephardic authorities note that such reference should be omitted. However, the *get* is valid if it is not omitted,[61] and some Sephardic authorities even favor keeping it so as to standardize bills of divorce.[62]

EH 130: SERVING AS A WITNESS

A *ger* may serve as a witness on a *get* just as he may serve as a witness in rabbinical court.[63] A *giyoret* may serve as a witness for any matter in which a Jewish woman may serve as a witness.

Laws of Levirate Marriage and Release

EH 157: NO LEVIRATE MARRIAGE (*YIBBUM*) OR LEVIRATE RELEASE (*CHALITZA*) FOR THE WIDOW OF A CHILDLESS *GER*

Since converts do not have, according to halacha, a father, a *ger* or Jewish man conceived before his mother converted has no levirate ties with his biological or maternal brother. A widow of one of them who dies childless is forbidden sexually to the other one (no *yibbum*)

---

60. EH 129:6, Taz, EH 129:7; Beit Shmuel, EH 129:39; Teshuvot Harosh 17:11; Tzitz Eliezer 21:1; Avnei Ha'ephod 17; Mishne Halachot 4:171.

61. KhG 40 at page 96 based on Yabai Omer EH 4:14.

62. See Pri Adama Volume 1, page 79b.

63. Chochmat Shlomo, EH 130:1; Ginat Vradim, Klal 1:1. However, using a technically incorrect although widespread name/designation (such as " [Hebrew name] son of [biological father])" can be problematic in a *get*.

and does not need to be released from levirate ties (no *chalitza*).[64]

However: two brothers conceived by Jewish parents (even if the parents are converts) are obviously fully related.[65]

EH 169: A *GER* MAY NOT SERVE ON A *BET DIN* FOR *CHALITZA*

Since the severing of levirate ties between a man and his childless brother's widow involves a mildly condemnatory designation of the man and his family,[66] an un-lineage *ger* and the still un-lineage son of converts may not serve on such a *bet din*.[67] (There is a debate over whether this restriction applies to the son of a born-Jew/ess and a convert.[68])

Laws of a Raped or Seduced Child

EH 171: THE RIGHTS OF A RAPED OR SEDUCED CHILD *GIYORET*

A *giyoret* who had converted as a baby or toddler[69] and was raped or seduced as a budding early adolescent (*na'arah*) virgin, is awarded the extra sum awarded to a child virgin when a rapist or seducer denies his guilt.[70] However, a child virgin *giyoret* who converted as a child older than a toddler does not collect the extra sum.[71]

---

64. Tur, YD 269; EH 157:3; Aruch Hashulchan, EH 157:6.

65. Yevamot 97b; EH 157:3.

66. Devarim 25:5.

67. Yevamot 102a. (As regards the debate over applying this limitation when he has lineage from his father and only his mother is a convert, see the supplemental essays.)

68. Rambam, Hilchot Yibum V'chalitza 4:5; Tur, EH 169; Terumat Hadeshen 226; Terumat Hadeshen, Letters 37; SA EH 169:2 and YD 269:11; Bach, EH 169:2–3; YD 269:11; Levush, EH Seder Chalitza 5; Beit Shmuel, EH 169:3; Aruch Hashulchan, EH 169:4.

69. Less than three years of age.

70. Since we no longer have rabbinic courts of *musmakhim*, contemporary courts only have the right to pressure the rapist to pay the sum instead of sending a court agent to forcibly collect the monies. (In any case, there is no country in the world with a functioning Jewish community in which rabbinical courts have the full powers of a state court.)

71. Ketuvot 36b, Rambam Issurei Biah 18:3, BY EH 177:1, Drisha EH 177:18. This needs further elaboration as to what is the halacha when this is factually false.

Choshen Mishpat

Rabbinic Courts • Loans • Oppressing/Cheating/Overpricing •
Gifts *Causa Mortis* • Objects Lost and Found • Inheritance •
Paying Monies Owed

Laws of Rabbinic Courts

CM 7: SERVING ON A *BET DIN* FOR MONETARY MATTERS

Wherever rabbinic courts have coercive jurisdiction, a *ger* may not
judge cases involving non-converts (see CM 8).[1] However, he may
judge non-converts in a voluntary court.[2]

CM 8: DISCRETIONARY AUTHORITY (*SERARA*)

Similar to the Biblical concern about the dynamics of, and injunction
against, appointing a foreigner as king,[3] the Talmudic rabbis understood that a convert also cannot serve as a king of Israel.[4] There is
some debate as to how far the concern over discretionary authority
(*serara*) applies to positions of governmental and communal authority.[5]

In any case, American Orthodox Judaism offers few positions of

---

1. Rambam, Hilchot Sanhedrin 2:9; Tur, CM 7; CM 7:2.
2. Tzitz Eliezer 19:47. The counterargument is that the *hazmana* process is
coercive. This approach seems to be incorrect in America, where a rabbinical
court has no authority unless the parties consent to attend. With consent, *serara*
is not a problem. Furthermore, no *hazmana* directs the use of any particular
rabbinical court; see Shulchan Aruch CM 1:3.
3. Devarim 17:15.
4. Kiddushin 72b.
5. See for example, Rambam Malachim 1:4.

discretionary authority.[6] As Rav Feinstein points out,[7] the American religious structure is essentially one of private and consensual institutions whose members can choose or displace their leaders and can easily choose to leave to a different institution. Thus, a convert can be a head of a *yeshiva* (*rosh yeshiva*), principal, *mashgiach*, community rabbi, *chazzan*, *gabbai*, *shochet*,[8] or synagogue president.[9] Indeed, yeshivot grant *semicha* to converts without any limitations.[10] Furthermore, Rav Moshe Feinstein notes that in light of the tension between the Talmudic rule against appointing a convert to matters of discretionary authority and the obligation to love the convert, all such questions should be resolved leniently whenever possible.[11]

However, there is a contemporary debate regarding religious public institutions in the State of Israel,[12] including but not limited to the positions of Chief Rabbi, rabbi of a city or town, and maybe even a military chaplain in the army; although the holder of the position is elected to the position for a fixed term, he has coercive power while in the position.

CM 26: THE PROHIBITION OF LITIGATING IN SECULAR COURT

When someone converts in the midst of litigating a conflict in sec-

---

6. Exceptions include being an *Admor* [rebbe of a Chasidic community]. An *Admor* has significant discretionary authority, and everyone who is affiliated with that community must obey him. His authority is supreme and not subject to any opposition or alternative.

7. See Igrot Moshe YD 4:26.

8. For further discussion of this issue, see Tzitz Eliezer 19:47; Teshuvot V'hanhagot 1:838, 3:305; Beit Mordechai 1:80; Hilchot Ketanot 1:39; Avnei Nezer, YD 313; Maharsham 4:107; Tzitz Eliezer 19:48.

9. See Bayai Chai CM 2 and 4, who permits a convert to be *parnass* for a community when the community selects him – and this is even more true in America where synagogue presidents have much less authority than they seem to have had in times of old. See similarly Ohel Yacov 4. But see Mishnah Halachot 15:99, who notes that appointing a convert as even a sexton is prohibited and certainly is prohibited as a rabbi or *rosh yeshiva*; see also KhG note 56 at page 125, who notes that this view is "not logical."

10. See "Orthodox Women Rabbis? Tentative Thoughts That Distinguish Between the Timely and the Timeless." *Hakirah, the Flatbush Journal of Jewish Law and Thought* 11 (2011), 25–58.

11. See Igrot Moshe, YD 4:26 regarding whether a convert may serve as the head of a *yeshiva*. See also Yashiv Yitzchak CM 1:46.

12. Cf. KhG 56 at page 123 note 56 who discusses public–private distinctions (but without mentioning Israel).

ular court with a Jew, it is preferable that they change venues to a rabbinic court (*bet din*) in line with the halacha that Jews adjudicate conflicts in *bet din*.[13]

CM 33: A CONVERT AS A WITNESS

As a Jew, a convert is permitted to serve as a witness for all matters that require suitable halachic witnessing, including marriage and divorce, and may witness contracts and documents of execution, such as a *get* and a *ketubah*.[14] A *giyoret* may serve as a witness for any matter that a Jewish woman may serve as a witness for.

A CONVERT'S CREDIBILITY ABOUT PRE-CONVERSION EVENTS

Although a convert may not later serve as the witness validating a Jewish marriage or divorce that the convert saw before converting, since such events require Jewish witnesses, the convert's testimony about pre-conversion events is believed if they knew enough to know what to observe and notice.[15] For example: the convert is believed regarding the *kashrut* of food that the convert purchased or prepared prior to conversion, and to identify the person who sold kosher *te-fillin*.[16]

BIOLOGICALLY RELATED CONVERTS WITNESSING AND TESTIFYING

Because converts are considered newly born, two converts who are biologically related may testify and witness for, or with, one another.[17] Twins conceived as non-Jews but born Jewish, however, may not do so because they are born maternal siblings of a Jewish mother.[18]

---

13. See Rabbi Yaakov Feit's excellent article "On the Matter of a *Heter Arkaot*," *Journal of the Beth Din of America* 1:30–48 (2012), which reasonably shows that it is appropriate to be strict in this matter. However, a counterargument is that there is no obligation to change venues since the secular litigation was halachically permitted when it began.

14. Chochmat Shlomo, EH 130:1; Ginat Vradim Klal 1:11.

15. Although CM 35:7 seems to rule the opposite, the ruling there refers to cases where formal witnessing is required or where he would not have known what he should be noticing (Hagahot Hagra, OC 39:4; Pri Megadim, Peticha to #32; Teshuvot Rabbi Akiva Eiger, Mahadura Kamma 4).

16. MHG 176.

17. Tur YD 269; Tur, CM 33; YD 269:10; CM 33:11; Radvaz 1:359.

18. Beit Yosef, CM 33:11; Sema 33:19; Shach, CM 33:7. See also Aruch

CM 34: REPENTANCE FROM PRE-CONVERSION SINS IN ORDER TO BE A VALID WITNESS

In spite of being newly born, a convert should repent for any pre-conversion violation of the seven Noachide Laws in order to be trusted as a witness, an element normally included in the process of conversion.[19]

Laws of Loan Debts

CM 67: THE SABBATICAL YEAR CANCELLATION OF LOAN DEBTS

It appears that *shemitta* does not cancel the loans made from or to a convert when they were not Jewish.[20] This is because the implicit condition of the loan was that it would not be subject to *shemitta* cancellation.[21]

CM 97: THE SIN OF PRESSURING OR EVEN PESTERING A MONEYLESS CONVERT TO REPAY A LOAN

Aside from the general prohibition to pester even by mere presence – let alone financially pressure – a moneyless debtor to repay a debt,[22] there is an extra prohibition to do so to a convert.[23]

Hashulchan, CM 33:8 though the limitation he proposes does not seem to be the normative halacha.

19. Birkei Yosef, CM 34:28; Shiurei Bracha, YD 269:1; Yalkut Yosef, CM Appendix 9. See also Rambam Melachim 10:4 who notes that there are situations where a convert can actually be punished for his pre-conversion sins.

20. Birur Halacha Hakatzar, CM 67:73; MHG 184.

21. See the Talmudic ruling codified in Rambam, Hilchot Shmitta V'yovel 9:10 that the terms of a loan can include a condition that the creditor will not cancel the debt during *shemitta*.

22. For a definition of moneyless, see CM 97:23.

23. Shemot 22:20; Rashi, Bava Metzia 59b; Rambam, Hilchot Mechira 14:15–16; Shulchan Aruch Harav CM, Ona'ah V'gneivat Daat 31. But see Imrei Kohen 13 for a discussion on whether this only applies to a poor convert. One must ask for repayment in a nice and gentle manner.

Laws of Oppressing, Cheating and Overpricing

CM 228: THE SIN OF CHEATING OR TORMENTING A CONVERT

There is a specific obligation to be careful to refrain from cheating or taunting a convert. This is above and beyond the general sin of cheating any person and of taunting one's fellow,[24] because cheating or tormenting a convert violates the additional biblical commandment to love the convert. This obligation applies even toward a convert who has stopped observing halacha[25] (even as all Jews have a difficult obligation to rebuke one another carefully over some sins), and all the more so forbids taunting a convert for any misconduct that they had engaged in as a Gentile.[26]

THE OBLIGATION TO REPAY THE DIFFERENTIAL, OR TO CANCEL, OVERPRICED SALES

As regards determining when the seller has an obligation to repay the differential of, or a buyer has a right to cancel, a transaction that had been priced over the market value: A transaction that was conducted when the convert was a Gentile is evaluated as a transaction with a Gentile.[27]

Laws of Gifting

CM 256: GIFTS *CAUSA MORTIS* (IN ANTICIPATION OF DEATH)

Just as a convert's children born before his conversion do not inherit from him by law, so a convert cannot orally gift to these children

---

24. CM 228:2.
25. See Imrei Kohen 13.
26. Bava Metzia 58b; Rambam, Hilchot Mechira 14:13; and Minchat Chinuch 431. One may mention his good deeds.
27. This flows from the formulation in CM 228.

causa mortis.[28] Rather, the convert who wishes to gift them must draw up a proper gifting will.[29] (Secular law might apply to this issue.)

Laws of Objects Lost and Found

CM 259: PROPERTY THAT A CONVERT FOUND OR LOST AS A GENTILE

A convert who converted from a Gentile culture that does not require finders to return objects found[30] is probably never obligated to return the lost object of a Jew that he found when he was a Gentile and had the right to acquire such objects.[31] However, a Jew might be required to return an object that a convert had lost as a Gentile because the mitzva to return an object found (*hashavat aveida*) now applies toward the convert.[32] Nevertheless, it is proper that both Jews and Gentiles

---

28. According to some authorities, this limitation always applies due to the concern that people might erroneously believe that children conceived as Gentiles receive inheritance benefits. Other authorities say that this limitation applies only when the convert has no Jewish children and that *causa mortis* oral gifts are only allowed for someone who has inheritors and decides to disburse some assets differently; it is not allowed to someone without inheritors – someone whose assets are available to all upon death.

29. Rif, Bava Batra 7a; Rambam, Hilchot Zechiya U'matana 9:7; Tur, CM 256; Beit Yosef, CM 256:1; CM 256:1; Rema CM 256:1; Aruch Hashulchan, CM 256:1, 5; Teshuvot HaRosh 15:1; Teshuvot HaRitva 79.

30. Since such conduct is legal and proper.

31. Chavot Ya'ir 79; MHG 183. The convert's right to maintain ownership may depend on whether the original Jewish owner had abandoned hope of reclaiming the object (*yiush*) before the finder's conversion (MLG note 21 on page 98).

32. Unless the Gentile abandoned hope of ever recovering the item (*yiush*). Nevertheless, as a general rule, one is automatically permitted to keep the lost object of a Gentile. The question of whether an object found by a "child convert" belongs to the convert or his father is related to the question of whether such a child is considered to be an orphan, in which case one may keep such objects, (CM 270:2) or as one with a father, in which case one may not (CM 270:2). MHG 183 is inclined to rule that the child is halachically considered to be an orphan, but this author thinks that it is more logical to rule in the other direction since the biological father does have some halachic recognition (see EH 23) and a secular legal obligation.

return all lost objects to their rightful owners even if one is not truly required to do so (*lifnim meshurat hadin*).[33]

CM 270: PROPERTY THAT A CHILD-CONVERT FOUND

If a convert child is supported by their Gentile or converted father, ownerless lost objects that such child finds belong to their father.[34]

Laws of Inheritance

CM 277: INHERITANCE OF THE FIRST SON BORN AFTER THE FATHER'S CONVERSION

If a *ger* already had a child that was conceived[35] before conversion, his first son born after the conversion is not considered a first born son who receives a double portion of the inheritance.[36] However, if the *ger* had children only with a Jewish woman before he converted, halacha does not consider the children to be his.[37] That means that if the first child born post-conversion is a boy, the boy is viewed as a first born son for the father and receives a double portion inheritance.[38]

CM 283: INHERITING FROM ONE'S GENTILE PARENTS

The rabbis decreed that, although a convert is considered a newborn, a convert inherits from their Gentile parents, lest converts return to

---

33. See for example, Shulchan Aruch CM 259:5.

34. Although the newborn child convert is fatherless in some senses and so could be viewed as an orphan who keeps objects found (MHG 183), the fact that halacha grounds the question of ownership in the reality of parental support (CM 270:2) points in the direction of granting ownership to the supportive biological father.

35. Sema CM 277:15.

36. CM 277:9; Sema CM 277:15; Aruch Hashulchan, CM 277:7.

37. This is because halacha considers the child of a Jewish woman and a Gentile man to be the Jewish child of the mother and not the Gentile child of the father (EH 4).

38. Netivot, 277:1; Aruch Hashulchan, CM 277:7.

their old faith in order to avoid losing the inheritance that would have been theirs had they remained Gentile.[39] However, as a newborn, a convert does not inherit from the Jewish father[40] who has the option to draw up a gifting will for the convert.

PRE-CONVERSION CHILDREN AND INHERITANCE

Those who were born to a *ger* before his conversion do not inherit from him[41] and can be gift-willed instead. A child who was conceived before their father converted also does not inherit from the biological father,[42] although it seems that they do inherit from the mother.[43]

ASSETS OF A CHILDLESS CONVERT WHO DIES

There is a rich compilation of Talmudic literature regarding the ownerless (*hefker*) assets of a convert who dies without children who were born after conversion. This discussion creates many fascinating hypotheticals in several aspects of commercial law, and is used as a tool to make analytic distinctions between various categories of properties. For the purposes of this book, however, we point out that the assets of an heirless convert should be disposed of in accordance with the convert's wishes; it is improper for anyone to seize the assets of a convert.[44] See also Appendix D.

---

39. CM 283:1.
40. Mishne Halachot 14:238.
41. CM 283:1.
42. CM 275:1.
43. See note 10, Hanhagot U'psakim Rav Yosef Chaim Zonnenfeld, Biurim Mammon V'kinyanim.
44. Aruch Hashulchan, CM 275:1.

Laws of Paying Monies Owed Before the Conversion

CM 359: CONTINUED OBLIGATION AFTER A CONVERSION TO PAY EARLIER DEBTS

A debt – of the principal of a loan[45] or for a breach of contract – between a Gentile and a Jew[46] remains in effect even after the Gentile party converts.[47]

CM 360: RETURNING OBJECTS STOLEN BEFORE CONVERSION

Although there is some discussion on the matter, a convert should return any object they still possess that had been stolen from a Jew when the convert was still a Gentile.[48]

CM 389: CONTINUED OBLIGATION AFTER CONVERSION TO PAY EARLIER TORT DAMAGES

Since a convert is obligated to pay debts incurred as a Gentile (above, CM 359), one is obligated to pay damage obligations that were incurred as a Gentile. Since a convert collects debts owed to them from before conversion, a convert receives compensation for torts suffered as a Gentile.[49]

---

45. Regarding the interest on a loan, read entry YD 171.
46. Regarding the interest on a loan, read entry YD 171.
47. See Sefer Chasidim 691; Chazon Ish, Bava Kamma 10:14; Chavot Ya'ir 49.
48. Maharsham 5:81:8; Chavot Yair 79; Yad Eliyahu 40. However, a *bet din* should not convert a Gentile who still has stolen objects in their possession.
49. Tosfot, Sanhedrin 71b s.v. ben noach; Chavot Yair 79. Although one might claim that this is disputed by the Rambam in Hilchot Melachim 10:4, this is not necessarily so. It appears to me that the Rambam there is simply making a jurisdictional claim that has nothing to do with financial liability.

Conclusion

Judaism aspires to welcome the convert as a member of the community of faithful. Thus, it is extremely important to ensure that members of our community not allow the faith to become a mere part of our genetic code that is exclusively passed down to those who are born-Jews. When a Gentile wishes to join the Covenant of Abraham, to nestle under the wings of the Almighty and to accept the yoke of Torah[50] as a righteous convert, it is the duty of the community to welcome them and help them in any and every way. This welcome is not only an abstract idea, but also a halachic duty. This duty sometimes even requires focusing on the convert in a way that might highlight the fact that the convert is alone and is in need of assistance when all others are with family, or even recognizing that people who previously were not Jewish and still have Gentile family face special situations. Indeed, sometimes these demands seem to push in more than one direction simultaneously, creating rules that can be nuanced and complex, reflecting a nuanced and complex reality with regard to a convert.

It is the goal of *A Concise Code of Jewish Law for Converts* to help ensure that the righteous convert finds their proper place within the community. Nothing is more appealing to the Almighty than that the convert be welcomed into the community.

---

50. The three-sided formulation invoked by Rambam in Issurai Biah 13:4.

Appendix A

Checklist of the transition rules that a convert encounters

This section collects in one place all of the rules related to the transition from a Gentile to a Jew. They are ordered in the sequence that a convert can readily follow the list upon conversion. No footnotes are cited here, and the reader, in order to understand these rules properly, should review them in the main work.

1. When a person converts, they should have a sense of the community of customs that they will follow.
2. At the time that a convert arises from the mikva, he or she blesses God for the mitzva of immersion (*al hatevila*).
3. According to Sephardic practice, the convert also blesses God for having lived to experience this event (*shehecheyanu*), while according to Ashkenazi practice they do not.
4. After the convert is dressed, it is the proper custom for the court to give the convert a Hebrew name and to bless God over a cup of wine.
5. Some Ashkenazi courts have the convert dress in a new garment, and bless God for having lived to experience this event (*shehecheyanu*).
6. On the day that a convert becomes Jewish, he or she is obligated in any daily commandment whose time has not yet passed at the moment of conversion. Even if performed that day as a Gentile, the convert must perform them again. Therefore, a *ger* who converts in the afternoon must don *tefillin* (the time frame of which is the entire day), bless God for the Torah (*birchot haTorah*), and pray the afternoon *mincha* service, but is exempt from the morning prayers and morning *kriat shema*.
7. One who converts in the afternoon is encouraged to refrain from eating before praying, similar to the general obligation to refrain from eating before praying first thing in the morning.
8. Regarding one who converts during the seven weeks between Pesach and Shavuot, there is a debate whether they are obligated

to count the remaining weeks and days of *sefirat ha'omer* and whether they should bless over the mitzva if they do count. This writer is of the view that a convert should count with a blessing.

9. A convert who converts after the initial holiday of a festival, during the weekdays of the festival (*chol hamo'ed*), should nonetheless immediately upon converting bless *shehechiyanu* for experiencing the festival.

10. A convert who converts on a fast day should fast.

11. A convert who converts on a delayed fast day need not fast.

12. A convert who immerses on Chanuka should kindle the appropriate number of lights with blessings on the remaining days since each night is its own mitzva, and should bless *shehechayanu* on the first night of kindling lights.

13. A convert who converts on Purim day is obligated in the daytime *megillah* reading.

14. As regards a three-day Purim weekend in Jerusalem (*Purim Meshulash*): if one converts on Friday, one is obligated in all of the mitzvot of Purim. If one converts on Sunday, one is obligated in none.

15. A convert may eat the food one cooked as a Gentile, but should not serve that food to other Jews.

16. A convert need not *kasher* their utensils if they had kept kosher since purchasing those utensils.

17. A convert must immerse their utensils upon conversion and perhaps should bless God over the mitzva (for those utensils for which a blessing is normally recited).

18. Open and not *mevushal* wine that had been handled earlier by no Gentiles other than the convert is not prohibited to them as a Jew, but is prohibited to other Jews as *stam yeinam*.

19. One who converts while he is a creditor or a debtor to a Jew on an interest bearing loan needs to closely read section YD (Yoreh Deah) 171 above.

20. As regards the principal of a loan and other general financial obligations – such as monies owed for tort, breach of contract, or theft – a convert must definitely pay monies owed and Jews must definitely repay monies owed.

21. A *giyoret* who menstruates before conversion does not have to wait seven clean days before being intimate with her remarried husband.

22. A *giyoret* calculates her period on the basis of her pre-conversion menses, since *vestot* are a biological phenomenon.

23. A convert should re-affix *mezuzot* on their doorposts after converting, now that they are obligated in the commandment.

24. A fertile woman who converts need not wait three months before remarrying if she takes a pregnancy test that reveals whether she is or is not pregnant. She may remarry her husband immediately, but, as every Jewess, must wait seven days before marrying a different man.

25. A convert couple who wishes to continue their marriage must remarry according to Jewish marriage laws. As any two single people, they may not be alone together until they remarry.

Appendix B

Converts and Jewish Law Related to the Temple or Messianic Times

Since this is a work of practical Jewish law, it does not collect all of the matters of Jewish law that are not relevant until the Temple is rebuilt. However, some are noted here.

1. One who converts in a time where the Temple exists is immediately obligated to bring a sacrifice as a new Jew.[1]
2. A convert who converts when no Temple exists but is still alive when the Temple is built has to consult the Jewish law authorities as to whether one needs to bring such a sacrifice.[2]
3. There are those who say that when the Temple exists a convert is rabbinically obligated after conversion to undergo the special Biblical process for purification from encountering human death.[3]
4. A *ger* is obligated in the triannual pilgrimage to the Temple (*aliyah l'regel*).[4]
5. It seems that a convert is obligated in the septennial popular assembly at the Temple to hear portions of the Torah read publicly (*hak'hel*).[5]
6. One who converts during the weekdays of a festival (*chol hamo'ed*), must still offer the festival (*chagiga*) sacrifice.[6]
7. A convert who converts between the eve of the central paschal

---

1. Keritut 9a. A claim could be made that one is not even Jewish until one brings the sacrifice (Rambam, Issurai Biah 13:1), but most *Rishonim* understand the sacrifice to be merely a post-conversion obligation (see Avnei Nezer YD 344 and Shut Chaim Shaul 1:80).
2. Since this is a matter of some dispute.
3. Pesachim 92a.
4. Noda B'Yehuda, tinyanah, OC 94, Shut Yachel Yisrael no. 31, Igrot Moshe OC 2:113.
5. Shut Minchat Yitzchak 10:153.
6. Jerusalem Talmud Chagiga 1:1, Avnei Nezer CM no. 128.

sacrifice of the Passover festival (*korban pesach rishon*) and the alternative paschal sacrifice a month later (*korban pesach sheini*) must offer the *pesach sheini*, since that date obligates those who due to duress had not offered the paschal sacrifice that year.[7]

8. It is unclear whether the non-circumcised sons of a *ger* prevent him from bringing the paschal *korban pesach*.[8]

9. Since a convert is considered newly born, on the one hand, but retains ownership of his original property, on the other hand, it is unclear whether one can offer an animal that was designated as a sacrifice when the convert was a Gentile.[9]

10. A *ger is* obligated in the annual half-*shekel* donation to the Temple.[10]

11. There is a dispute whether a farmer *ger* – a person who has no portion in the land of Israel as formally divided by lineage – joins other farmers in declaring on the fourth and seventh years of the seven-year agricultural cycle that he had indeed tithed all his produce (*vidui ma'asrot*).[11]

12. There is a dispute whether a *ger* may be sold as an indentured servant (*eved ivri*).[12]

13. A convert cannot serve on a court (*bet din*) in a capital case.[13]

14. A *giyoret* repeatedly caught in suspected adulterous seclusion can drink the testing *sotah* waters.[14] A *ger's* wife repeatedly caught in suspected adulterous seclusion can also drink the testing *sotah* waters.[15]

---

7. Pesachim 93a, Rambam Hilchot Korban Pesach 5:7, Shut Birkat Avraham no. 4, Shut Levush Mordechai first edition no. 222.

8. Rashi, Tosafot Yevamot 48a, Shut Tzitz Eliezer 2:11.

9. MhG 174.

10. Rambam Shekalim 1:7.

11. Mishnah Ma'aser Sheni 5:13, Shut Sha'ar Ephraim no. 14, Rambam MT Hilchot Ma'aser Sheni 11:17.

12. Bava Metzia 71a.

13. BY YD 269:11, since this is a matter of community and invokes almost divine authority.

14. Rambam Sotah 2:6.

15. Shut Emunat Shmuel no. 7.

Appendix C

Rules for the son or daughter carried by a pregnant woman who converts to Judaism

There is a dispute whether a child who had been conceived when his mother was a Gentile but was born Jewish due to the mother's conversion while pregnant,[1] is a Jew from birth or a born convert. One school of thought claims that this child is a Jew from birth as the child of a Jewish mother.[2] The other school of thought avers that this child was converted as a fetus.[3] In practice, such a child is subject to the following rules:

1. Regardless of the debate, the child's birth mother is considered the mother of this child for matters of Jewish law. If twins are born they are considered maternal siblings.[4] Moreover, the child is forbidden by Torah law to marry all of his mother's relatives (and by rabbinic decree all of his father's relatives[5]).
2. Regardless of the debate, the child cannot opt out of Judaism as can a child convert (according to many).[6]
3. According to the second view, such a daughter may not marry a

---

1. Yevamot 78a.

2. The Beit Yosef commenting on Tur EH 6; see Sema CM 33:19.

3. The Chelkak Mechokek 6:10 and 7:29 (and Shach 33:7). Berchai Yosef CM 33:4, who notes that the view of the Beit Yosef is rejected. For more on this dispute, see Piskei Din Jerusalem dinei mamanut uberuray Yehadut, 4:321.

Within this group there is an even smaller group that thinks that such a circumcision needs to be performed in front of a rabbinical court for the sake of conversion (Mishnat Hager page 111). However, this is generally not followed and is not logical – since this child is viewed as either simply born to a Jewish mother or as already converted *in utero* when circumcision was not necessary. So too, this child cannot retract his conversion; Teferet Lemoshe 268 sv *beshulchan aruch*. See Pitchai Teshuva 268:8.

4. Yevamot 97b and parallels. YD 269:4.

5. Yevamot 98a, Shut Shevet Ha-Levi 3:207.

6. Tiferet Lemoshe YD 268:6 as cited in PT YD 268:8 and Avnei Miluim 4:2.

Kohen (with possible exceptions).[7] Even according to the first view, the debate over whether a daughter of two converts may marry a Kohen[8] would apply here.

4. Some rule that such a son is circumcised on the eighth day, even on Shabbat,[9] while others rule that he should not be circumcised on Shabbat.[10] Contemporary practice seems to be to refrain from Shabbat circumcisions.[11]

---

7. See Chelkak Mechokek 6:10 and 7:29 Shach 33:7; Berchai Yosef CM 33:4; and Tzitz Eliezer 17:47. But Kovetz Shiurim of Rabbi Elchanan Wasserman 2:11 notes that when the immersion takes place within the first forty days of pregnancy the child is a born Jewess and may marry a Kohen. See also Piskei Din Jerusalem on Financial and Jewish matters 4:321. See also Rabbi Yaacov Ariel, *meuberet shenitgar'a Techumin* 20:251–260 (5760), who uses Rabbi Elchanan Wasserman's ruling as one grounds of many to allow her to marry a Kohen.

8. See Shulchn Aruch EH 7:21. For more on this, see "Who is a ger" at http://www.torahmusings.com/2012/11/who-is-a-ger/. And see the supplemental essay in the book, "The Children of Two Converts: Are They Considered *Gerim*?"

9. See Shut Maharam Shick 247 and Letters of Rabbi Chaim Ozer Grodzinski 27 – both of whom note that the practice is to do the mila on Shabbat.

10. Rabbi Yaakov Emden, Migdal Oz Mila, Nachal 7:3, Shut Binyan Tzion 22.

11. Rabbi Shlomo Zalman Auerbach Halacha Verefuah 5:81 notes to be strict. Conversations with *mohalim* confirm that to be the practice.

Appendix D

There is a rich compilation of Talmudic literature regarding the assets of a convert who dies with no relatives, and thus their assets become ownerless, or *hefker*. This discussion creates many fascinating hypotheticals in many aspects of commercial law, and is a tool widely used to make analytic distinctions between various categories of properties, since this is nearly the only way property can become ownerless as a matter of Jewish law without someone abandoning it. This section will only briefly summarize the rules that obtain for a convert.

As a matter of normative Jewish law, the assets of a convert who dies should be disposed of consistent with their valid will and secular law.[1] However, the default halachic rules are as follows:

Economic Matters

1. A convert who dies with no Jewish family leaves assets ownerless as a matter of theory and anyone who takes possession of them owns them.[2] This is true even if the convert has children who converted with them,[3] unless one gifted assets to them properly. Thus:
    *   An heirless convert's slaves (in times that this was permitted and done, and not during our days) go free after the convert dies (unless they are minors, in which case others can seize them).[4]

---

1. Aruch HashulchanCM 275:1.
2. SA CM 275:1.
3. See comments of Kennesset Hagedolah on CM 275.
4. YD 267:65.

- Collateral held by an heirless convert-creditor at the time of death returns to the debtor-owner of the collateral.[5]
- Those who physically possess items owed to an heirless convert own them at the time of death.[6]
- In general: objects held by others at the time of an heirless convert's death are owned by them.[7]
- In fact, when an heirless convert business partner of another Jew dies, it seems that someone else can take possession of the convert's place as partner in the assets and venture; the Jewish partner does not own the deceased convert's half of the business unless they grab the assets.[8]

Moreover, although it is of course prohibited to steal from a convert as long as they are alive:[9]

- Someone who owed, but did not pay an heirless convert, for causing the convert's wife to miscarry no longer has to pay for the loss of the fetus after death of such a convert.[10]
- If someone's ox gores an heirless convert to death, it is unclear who gets the penalty money.[11]
- In general, someone who owed a penalty to an heirless convert who dies before payment is exempt from payment.[12]

Note: The convert may retain a basic right to their assets; there is a dispute whether those who seize the deceased heirless convert's assets need to pay for the deceased convert's funeral (or the community as a whole needs to provide them with a minimal funeral).[13]

2. However, although the death of an heirless convert also ends their monetary obligations to others,[14] the creditors do have rights:

---

5. Tur CM 72, SA CM 72:36–37, 275:2, Levush CM 275:27, Ketzot 66:27, AH CM 72:62.

6. Tur CM 127, BY CM 127:2, Darchei Moshe CM 66:11, SA CM 66:37, 127:2, Tumim CM 66:15, AH CM 127:2 and CM 275:28.

7. Shut Rashba 2:252.

8. Sha'ar Mishpat 275:1.

9. Tur CM 367, SA CM 367:6, Aruch Hashulchan 367:2.

10. Bach CM 423:2, SA CM 423:2, Aruch Hashulchan423:4.

11. Shut Chatam Sofer 4:149.

12. Aruch HashulchanCM 405:3, 7.

13. SA CM 275:2, AH CM 275:1.

14. CM 66:37; 127:2; 275:27, Bach CM 72:32, Sha'ar Mishpat 245:1, 348:3, Avnei Miluim 102:1, AH CM 275:29, 31.

- If a convert dies, his wife can collect her *ketubah* from his property.[15]
- An heirless convert-debtor's collateral held by creditor at the time of the convert's death belongs to the creditor.[16]
- People who seize the ownerless property have to pay the convert's creditors the value of the property seized.[17] (There is an elaborate literature about whose debts get priority: most Jewish law authorities think this is governed by secular law.[18])
- However, debts that a convert sold to others remain owned by those creditors,[19] as are contracts (both for sales and loans).[20]

Ritual Law

3. Since the property of a deceased heirless convert is ownerless:
    - If an heirless convert dies on Friday, their property prohibits all residents of the courtyard to use the courtyard unless the person who takes possession of the property cancels the right to carry in the area in order to allow everyone else to carry in the area.[21]
    - If an heirless convert dies on Pesach without managing to destroy their *chametz*, nobody is obligated to destroy it.[22] Moreover, if some such convert dies before Pesach (even early the day before, before *chametz* becomes forbidden), their *chametz* is permitted to be consumed after Pesach

---

15. Shut Rashba 2:252.

16. Tur CM 72, BY CM 72:39, CM 194:2, CM 275:28, SA CM 72:39, Urim CM 127:4, Avnei Miluim 102:1, AH CM 72:66 and CM 275:29.

17. Rambam Zechiya U'matanah 2:17, SA CM 275:31, Ketzot 111:1–2.

18. SA CM 275:28 and 31.

19. Tumin CM 66:43, Avnei Miluim 105:2, Aruch Hashulchan CM 66:45, Shut Maharshdam CM no. 64.

20. Bava Bara 54b, Shach CM 275:3, Ketzot 66:10, Shut Divrei Rivot no. 342.

21. Mishna Eruvin 6:3–4; Rambam MT Eruvin 2:1; Sh"A OH 371:5; AH and MB there.

22. Shut Noda B'Yehuda first edition OC no. 15.

since it did not become forbidden on Pesach as *chametz* owned by a Jew.[23]

- If an animal of an heirless convert gives birth after the owner dies, the rule of the first born animal (*bechor*) does not apply to it.[24]

23. Mishbitzot Zahav OC 448:7, Eishel Avraham OC 443:1, Birkei Yosef YD 281, MB 448:2; Aruch Hashulchan OC 448:3.

24. Shut Chatam Sofer 2:315, 317.

עיונים בהלכות גרים

Supplemental Essays
on the Laws of Converts

Supplemental Essays

There are four supplemental essays presented here, each of which elaborates on an important theme mentioned in previous sections. These essays are intended for the reader who wants to dive more deeply into these themes. They are intended to help the reader understand these halachic issues by reviewing and analyzing a range of rabbinic opinions – including positions not followed. The essays are sometimes complex.

The first essay (co-authored with Rabbi Dr. Mark Goldfeder, an erudite colleague at Emory University School of Law) focuses on the issue of what blessing a convert should bless in the morning when born-Jews bless *shelo asani goy* (who did not make me a Gentile). This essay reviews rabbinic views concerning the texts of prayers as it focuses on this blessing of identity.

The second essay is entitled "May a Convert be a Member of a Rabbinical Court for Conversion?" It focuses on the role of converts in the rabbinical courts generally, and then focuses on the particularly difficult case of a convert performing other conversions. Many issues are discussed in this essay, including the question of *serarah* (power and authority), the nature of conversion, and how to resolve hard disputed matters of Jewish law.

The next essay discusses the status of a child born to two converts who marry. It is an attempt to explain why and for which matters some Jewish law authorities rule that this child has aspects of being a convert.

The final essay is entitled "May the Daughter of a Gentile Man and a Jewish Woman Marry a Kohen?" While it focuses on that problem, it also serves as a basic review of Jew-Gentile marital relations and of the status of a person whose father is a Gentile but mother is Jewish.

In short, these essays provide important background to anyone who wants to consider more deeply the important issues that were mentioned in the Code. These essays help frame those important issues.

Shelo Asani Goy:
What *Bracha* Does a *Ger* Bless?

**(This essay was jointly written
with Rabbi Dr. Mark A. Goldfeder of Emory University)**

Introduction

This article examines one modern question related to converts and prayer: What is the proper identity blessing that a convert should bless in the daily morning service? Can he or she bless any or all of the following different formulations: "*shelo asani goy*" ("who did not make me a non-Jew"), "*she'asani ger*" ("who made me a convert"), "*she'asani yehudi*," ("who made me a Jew"); should they skip the blessing entirely; or is there some different *bracha* that they should in fact bless? Depending on which blessing they choose, what are the consequences for the other *berachot* that are usually blessed at that point in *shacharit*? Should the answer be different for the convert who leads the congregation as the *shaliach tzibbur*?

This article is divided into five sections: (I) The first section surveys both the only explicit discussion of this topic in the literature of the medieval rabbinic Rishonim, the Ramah's[1] discussion, and the interpretations of that discussion by the early modern rabbinic authorities, Beit Yosef and Rema, in their commentaries on the Tur code of law. (II) The second section explores how this issue is codified in the Shulchan Aruch code of law and in its classical commentators. (III) The third section explores contemporary rabbinic decisors' (*poskim*'s) takes on this topic, while (IV) the fourth section lists other suggestions and formulations that have been made over the generations. (V) The conclusion summarizes the various views while offering some practical halachic recommendations.

---

1. Meir ben Todros HaLevi Abulafia (c. 1170–1244, Burgos, Spain).

A. THE TALMUDIC BLESSING AND THE PROBLEM IDENTIFIED BY THE AVUDRAHAM FOR A CONVERT

As part of the morning prayers it is incumbent upon every Jewish individual to bless a series of identity blessings (*berachot*). As the Talmud in Menachot 43b recounts:[2]

תניא, היה ר"מ אומר: חייב אדם לברך שלש ברכות בכל יום, אלו הן: שעשאני ישראל, שלא עשאני אשה, שלא עשאני בור. רב אחא בר יעקב שמעיה לבריה דהוה קא מברך שלא עשאני בור, אמר ליה האי כולי האי נמי? אמר ליה: ואלא מאי מברך? שלא עשאני עבד.

Rabbi Meir used to say: A man is required to bless three blessings every day, and these are: "[Blessed are You] who has made me a Jew; [Blessed are You] who has not made me a woman; [Blessed are You] who has not made me an empty person . . . Rav Acha bar Yaakov replaces the last with 'who has not made me a slave.'"

In the wording of *siddurim* from the last many hundreds of years and of living traditions, these three identity blessings are commonly formulated as follows: *shelo asani goy*,[3] *shelo asani eved*, and *shelo asani isha*

---

2. Following the text of the standard Vilna edition.

3. There is an extensive literature regarding the version of this *beracha*. The formulation of the Pri Megadim (OC Mishbetzot Zahav 46:5), the Magen Avraham (OC 46:9), and the Taz (OC 46:4,6) is *shelo asani oveid kochavim*, literally "who has not made me an idol worshipper." There are those who question this formulation due to changing social circumstances; while it may have been the case in the time of the Talmud that the average non-Jew was worshipping idols, nowadays many non-Jews do not fall into this category, and so the blessing would not be inclusive enough in terms of differentiating us from non-Jewish people. In addition, even the word *goy* as used by the Rambam (and as found in our versions of the Tosefta and Yerushalmi) to describe a Gentile is not precise enough for some; the word *goy* can be used to describe *any* nation, including (over 60 times in Scripture) the Jewish people themselves. Thus, the version found in the Machzor Vitri and in the Shulchan Aruch Harav has *shelo asani nachri* (lit. "Who has not made me a stranger") and some Jews of German descent have adopted this terminology, in their view a more exact description for a person that is not of Jewish lineage. It does not, however, entirely avoid the problems of vagueness either, as *nachri* in the Torah can also refer to a Jewish person from a different family. In fact, scripturally the word *nachri* is only used to refer to a non-Jew when it is directly paired in context with a reference to a Jew, i.e., Devarim 17:15. The Vilna Gaon, in his commentary to OC 46:4, notes that, while the Rif and Rambam have the language of *shelo asani goy*, "in our books, the language of the Talmud is *sheasani yisrael, and so it is in the Rosh and the Tur*" (emphasis added).

(respectively, "Blessed are You . . . Who has not made me a Gentile, a slave, or a woman") – while women commonly substitute *"sheasani kirtzono"* ("Who has made me in accordance with His will") for the last blessing.[4]

The Talmud and the *siddurim*, however, do not tell us what identity blessing a convert blesses in the morning. It was the leading authority of the early history of High Medieval Spanish Jewry, the Ramah,[5] who first answered this question explicitly in the following manner (as transmitted in the Sefer Avudraham, a miniature code of prayer and blessings):

נשאל הרמ"ה אם יכול לברך גר שלא עשני גוי. ושבוי שלא עשני עבד והשיב: כך ראינו שאין הברכה אלא על תחלת ברייתו של אדם לפיכך אין הגר מברך שלא עשני גוי אלא כל זמן שהורתו ולידתו בקדושה

> They asked the Ramah if a convert is able to bless "who has not made me a Gentile," or [whether] a captive [is able to bless] "who has not made me a slave." And he answered: Thus we have seen. The blessing refers to the initial creation of a person. Therefore, the convert cannot bless *shelo asani goy*, unless one were conceived and born in holiness [i.e., by an already Jewish mother].[6]

Sefer Orchot Chaim (Hilkhot Meah Brachot, 8) and the Avudraham concur with the Ramah.[7]

The position of the Ramah is analytically clear and simple to un-

---

Interestingly, while this positive formulation is the version in our Talmud, in our editions of the Rosh and the Tur the negative formulation of *shelo asani goy* is used. This leads to the not impossible hypothesis that the original texts were subject to a late editorial emendation, wherein the one positive formulation laid out for recitation (*sheasani yisrael*) was changed to be more in line with the other two (negative) blessings. Indeed from the language and reasoning of the Tur (OC 46) ("he says this *bracha* because he needs to give praise and thanks to God who chose us from all the idol worshippers and brought us close to his service") the positive formulation seems like it might be a better contextual fit.

4. While, as noted above, there is a tremendous literature on what the correct text of the blessing for all Jews should be, the near-universal custom has been for natural-born Jews to make the blessing of *shelo asani goy*, *akkum* or *nachri* (variant words that mean Gentile).

5. Meir ben Todros HaLevi Abulafia (c. 1170–1244, Burgos, Spain).

6. Sefer Avudraham, Birchot Hashachar (p. 41) (David ben Josef ben David Abudirham, Spain, fl. 1340).

7. Sefer Avudraham, Birchot Hashachar (p. 41) (David ben Josef ben David Abudirham, Spain, fl. 1340).

derstand. A person may not bless God inaccurately. Were a convert to bless God for not having been created a Gentile, he would in fact be stating a patent falsehood. Thus the convert must skip this blessing.

However, Ramah's older contemporary and apogee of Muslim Jewry (including southern Spanish Jewry) – the Rambam – ruled otherwise as regards converts and blessings in general. In his famous letter to Rabbi Ovadia the Convert, Rambam writes:

יש לך לומר הכל כתקנן ואל תשנה דבר, אלא כמו שיתפלל ויברך כל אזרח
מישראל כך ראוי לך לברך ולהתפלל בין שתתפלל יחידי בין שתהיה שליח צבור,
ועיקר הדבר שאאע"ה הוא שלימד כל העם וכו' לפיכך כל מי שנתגייר עד סוף
כל הדורות וכל המייחד שמו של הקב"ה כמו שהוא כתוב בתורה מתלמידיו של
אברהם אבינו ע"ה הוא וכו' נמצא אברהם אבינו ע"ה הוא אב לזרעו הכשרים
ההולכים בדרכיו ואב לתלמידיו והם כל גר שיתגייר, לפיכך יש לך לומר או"א
אבותינו שאברהם אבינו ע"ה הוא אביך, ויש לך לומר שהנחלת את אבותינו
שלאברהם נתנה הארץ שנא' לו קום התהלך בארץ לארכה ולרחבה כי לך אתננה,
אבל שהוצאתנו ממצרים או שעשית נסים לאבותינו, אם רצית לשנות ולומר
שהוצאת את ישראל ממצרים ושעשית נסים לישראל אמור, ואם לא שנית אין
בכך הפסד כלום.

You should say everything in the prescribed order and not change anything. Rather just like every Jew (by birth) says their blessings and prayers, so too it is fitting for you to bless and pray alike, whether you are praying alone or leading the congregation. And the main reason for this is that Abraham our father is the one who taught the people, opened their minds, and revealed to them the true faith and the unity of God; he rejected the idols and abolished their adoration; he brought many children under the wings of the Divine Presence; he gave them counsel and advice, and ordered his sons and the members of his household after him to keep the ways of the Lord forever, as it is written, "For I have known him to the end that he may command his children and his household after him, that they may keep the way of the Lord, to do righteousness and justice" (Gen. 18:19). Therefore whoever converts, until the end of the generations, and whoever confesses the unity of the Divine Name as it is prescribed in the Torah, is counted among the disciples of Abraham our father, peace be with him . . . Therefore Abraham our father, peace be with him, is the father of his pious posterity who walk in his ways, and the father of his disciples, and they are all proselytes who adopt Judaism. Therefore you should pray, "Our God and the God of our fathers," for Abraham our father, peace be with him, he is your father. And you should say, "You who have taken for Your own our fathers," for the land was given to Abraham, as it was said to him, "Arise, walk through the land in the length of it and in the breadth of it; for to you I will give it." But as to the words, "that You have brought us out of Egypt" or "that You who have done miracles for our fathers" – if you want to change these, and say, "that You who have brought Israel out of the land of Egypt" and "that You who have done miracles to Israel," you may say this. If, however, you do not change them, there is no loss in it.[8]

Rambam notes that in regard to historical assertions a convert does not have to change anything but is allowed some leeway if he desires to be more accurate. As Rambam explains, the prayers and blessings are "prescribed" for all Jews and need not be modified to make note of specific and unusual circumstances.

In spite of the implications of this letter, Rabbi Yosef Karo – the leading 15th century codifier of post-exilic Spanish Jewry – quotes

---

8. Responsa of Rambam 293. It is also cited in full in Tzitz Eliezer 17:42. The Rambam continues, proving his point as follows:

וכל מה שאמרנו לך בענין הברכות שלא תשנה כבר ראיה לזה ממסכת בכורים תמן תנינן הגר מביא ואינו קורא שאינו יכול לומר אשר נשבע י"י לאבותינו לתת לנו. וכשהוא מתפלל בינו לבין עצמו אומר או"א אבות ישראל. וכשהוא מתפלל בבית הכנסת אומר או"א אבותינו זהו סתם משנה. והיא לר' מאיר ואינה הלכה (הל' בכורים פ"ד הל' ג') אלא כמו שנתפרש בירושלמי תמן אמרינן תני בשם ר' יהודה גר עצמו מביא וקורא מאי טעמיה כי אב המון גוים נתתיך לשעבר היית אב לאברהם מכאן ואילך אב לכל הבריות. ר' יהושע בן לוי אמר הלכה כר' יהודה. אתא עובדא קמיה דר' אבהו והורי כר' יהודה. הנה נתברר לך שיש לך לומר אשר נשבע י"י לאבותינו לתת לנו. ושאברהם אב לך ולנו ולכל הצדיקים ללכת בדרכיו והוא הדין לשאר הברכות והתפלות שלא תשנה כלום.

And all that we said to you in regard to the blessings, that you should not change anything, here is already a proof to this from Tractate Bikkurim. There we learned in a mishnah: The *ger* brings (first fruits) but does not read (the accompanying declaration), because he is not able to say the phrase "that God promised to our forefathers to give to us." And when he prays by himself, he says, "The God of the forefathers of Israel," and when he prays in the synagogue he says, "Our God and the God of our forefathers," This is an unattributed (*stam*) mishnah, which represents the view of Rabbi Meir, and is not the halacha, rather it is as is explained in the Talmud Yerushalmi. There we say, "We learned in a *baraita* in the name of Rabbi Yehuda 'a convert himself brings and reads the declaration.' What is his reason? [Because God said to Abraham], 'For I have made you father of many nations.' In the past you were the father to [the descendants of] Abraham, from here onward you are the father for all the beings. Rabbi Yehoshua Ben Levi said the halacha is like Rabbi Yehuda. A case came before Rabbi Abahu, and he ruled like Rabbi Yehuda. Behold it is revealed to you that you should say 'that God promised our forefathers to give to us,' and that Abraham is a father to us and to all of the righteous people, to go in his ways. And so it is the law in regard to the rest of the *brachot* and *tefillot*, that you (R' Ovadia Ger) should not change anything.

and seems to agree with the Ramah's position as rendered in the Avudraham code of prayer. In his Beit Yosef commentary on the Tur Code of Jewish Law (OC 46), Rabbi Yosef Karo states as follows:

וכתב ה"ר דוד אבודרהם שהשיב הרמ"ה שברכות אלו אינם אלא על תחלת
בריאתו של אדם לפיכך הגר אינו מברך שלא עשני גוי כל שלא היתה הורתו
ולידתו בקדושה.

Rabbi David Avudraham writes that the Ramah answered that these blessings refer to the initial creation of a person. Therefore, the convert does not bless *shelo asani goy*, unless one were conceived and born in holiness [i.e., by an already Jewish mother].

The debate does not end there, however. Rabbi Yosef Karo's famous Polish Ashkenazic contemporary – Rabbi Moshe Isserles (Rema) – offers a third alternative. In his Darchei Moshe HaAruch commentary on the Tur (Orach Chaim 46:3), Rema posits that a convert can formulate a more accurate blessing:

ונראה הגר יכול לברך שעשני גר דזה נמי מיקרי עשייה כמו שנאמר (בראשית יב ה)
ואת הנפש אשר עשו בחרן:

It appears that a convert can make the blessing "Who made me a convert (*sheasani ger*)" because this [act of converting] is also called *asiyah* [creating].

The Rema accepts the medieval Ramah's argument that a convert cannot falsely bless "who did not make me a Gentile," but proposes that the convert bless God instead for having made him a convert.

A generation later, however, the Bach – a student of the Rema's leading student – disagreed with the Rema's assertion that conversion constitutes a creation.[9] He therefore concludes in his own commentary on the Tur that a convert has to omit this blessing entirely since it is no truer that God made someone a convert than that God had made a convert a Jew from birth.[10]

Thus, from the commentaries on the Tur we see two views:
- Beit Yosef and Bach rule that the convert should skip the blessing.
- Rema rules that a convert should say a new and novel blessing: "who made me a convert."

---

9. This is also mentioned by the Magen Avraham (OC 46:9).
10. Bach OC 46:7.

The Rambam's view is not addressed.

B. THE SHULCHAN ARUCH, REMA, AND COMMENTATORS

In Rabbi Karo's Shulchan Aruch Code, a short review code for his encyclopedic Beit Yosef, Rabbi Karo ignored the question of what blessing the convert should make (OC 46:4). Rema in his glosses to the Shulchan Aruch, however, does not ignore the question. Unfortunately, his gloss seems to make no sense. The Shulchan Aruch with the Rema's gloss as found in the edition widely used today[11] reads as follows:

צריך לברך בכל יום: שלא עשני עובד כוכבים . . .

A person is required to bless every day: Who did not make me an idol worshipper . . .

הגה: ואפי' גר היה יכול לברך כך אבל לא יאמר: שלא עשני עכו"ם, שהרי היה עכו"ם מתחלה

[Rema's] Gloss: And even a convert can bless this way. But he should not say "Who did not make me an idol worshipper," because they were an idol worshipper at first.

On the face of it, the comment of the Rema simply makes no sense; what does it mean to say that a convert can bless this way if immediately after he says that, a convert cannot bless the standard blessing of "who did not make me an idol-worshipper"?

The answer to this question is found in the fact – pointed out by the editors of the excellent Machon Yerushalayim edition of the Shulchan Aruch[12] – that the edition that the Rema used when he originally wrote his glosses was not the original 1565 Venice edition (which we quoted), but rather the Kavli edition published two years later, in 1567. In the Kavli 1567 edition of the Shulchan Aruch – the one that the Rema saw and on which he commented – the beracha that Rabbi Karo rules that people must bless is the positive formulation of the blessing, *sheasani yehudi*.[13] Thus the Rema's original gloss reads as follows:

---

11. The version typeset in Vilna in 1895 on the basis of the 1565 first edition of the Shulchan Aruch from Venice.

12. Shulchan Aruch, Orach Chaim. Jerusalem: Machon Yerushalayim, 1997/98.

13. See also the notes in the Tur OC 46 (Shirat Devorah edition), note 12*.

צריך לברך בכל יום: שעשני יהודי . . .

A person is required to bless every day: "Who made me a Jew"

הגה: ואפי' גר היה יכול לברך כך אבל לא יאמר: שלא עשני עכו"ם, שהרי היה
עכו"ם מתחלה

And even a convert can bless this way [of saying she'asani yehudi].
But one should not say "Who did not make me an idol worshipper,"
because they were an idol worshipper at first.

Rema thinks that everyone – including a convert – may bless *she'asani yehudi* since the convert was made a Jew through conversion. But Rema recognizes that there are those who state *shelo asani goy* ("who did not make me a Gentile") and insists that a convert may not bless in that formulation since it is simply false.

The Levush (46:5), the Birkei Yosef (46:9), the Yafeh Lileiv (46:6), and the Maamar Mordechai (46:7) all note that they too have seen this original Shulchan Aruch of Kavli 1567 and rule accordingly: The convert may bless *she'asani yehudi* (presumably for the same reason that the Rema allowed blessing *she'asani ger* in his Darchei Moshe) but should not bless *shelo asani goy* inasmuch as they were originally a Gentile. Even the Bach (OC 46), discussed above, who argues that conversion is not in fact a creation and thus rejects the Rema's ruling, understands the Rema in this manner.

Moreover, even the commentators on the Shulchan Aruch who are unaware of (or ignore)[14] this answer – such as the Magen Avraham,[15] the Biur Hagra,[16] and the Mishnah Berurah[17] – simply assume that what the Rema meant to say here is what he said in the Darchei

---

14. Rabbi Dr. Aryeh Frimer – who is troubled by the fact that, although the variant bracha formulation of *sheasani yisroel/yehudi* does appear early on, it is not as attested to in the tradition as *shelo asani goy* is – notes that there were clear acts of censorship at play when these texts were being written and suggests (as does the Torat Chaim) that the Rema knew that the text of *sheasani yisrael* in his Shulchan Aruch was a censor's modification and simply ignored that version when he wrote his gloss. Although we find this specific suggestion hard to believe (in contrast to his many insightful suggestions on this paper which he graciously gave of his own time via emails), we will see – in any case – that there is no significant difference between these readings of the Rema.

15. SA OC 46:10.

16. SA OC 46:4.

17. OC 46:18.

Moshe; he meant to say that a convert also blesses a form of this blessing – and that form is *she'asani ger*.[18]

Theoretically, one could discern a slight difference between these understandings of the Rema. According to the latter position, the Rema always ruled that a convert should bless *she'asani ger*. According to the first position, the Rema in his glosses to the Shulchan Aruch – written after his Darchei Moshe – has a convert bless *she'asani yehudi*. However, both understandings agree that the Rema forbids a convert to bless God with the formulation of *shelo asani goy* – which would be a lie – and permits formulating an accurate version of the blessing.[19] Moreover, since the Rema did not feel particularly wedded to the Talmudic formulation of the identity blessing (as evidenced by the fact that he felt comfortable advocating that a convert bless *she'asani ger*, a Talmudically unsupported formulation), there is no reason to conclude that he would have felt less comfortable with a convert blessing *she'asani yisrael* than with a convert blessing *she'asani ger*[20] – especially in communities in which everyone blesses *she'asani yisrael*. In other words, there is no practical difference between these two understandings since Rema accepts a formulation of an identity blessing as long as it is both accurate and conveys the same general idea.[21]

---

18. Admittedly, the Shlah (Shlah Chullin, Perek Derekh Hayyim Tohakhat Mussar 231) opines that this gloss is a later addition and a forgery. However, the evidence suggests that this simply is not true. Not only did the earliest commentators – including the Rema's student, Levush (46:5) – assume that the Rema meant *something* with his comment, but this gloss is also found in the first edition of the Rema's glosses (Krakow, 1570). See http://www.hebrewbooks.org /45673 for a copy of that first edition.

19. See Machon Yerushalayim notes to the Shulchan Aruch OC 46:4, where this observation is made quite clearly.

20. See Levush OC 46:5 who seems to adopt this view.

21. To elaborate: In line with halachic tradition that had allowed adding identity blessings not found in the Talmud – such as *sheasani kirtzono* and *hanoten layef koach* – the Rema understood that the point of these blessings – as the Talmud notes – is to help a person get up to 100 blessings a day through praises that relate to his being and existence. As the Taz (OC 46:4) wrote two generations later about women reciting the blessing of *sheasani kirtzono*: "It seems to me that the reason women may recite the blessing of 'who has made me according to his will,' even though this blessing is not in the Gemara, is based on what I wrote earlier: it is permissible because it can be deduced from the man's blessing that there is some benefit in being a woman, therefore she should offer thanks for her own good qualities. This seems to me a correct explanation." (Cf. Tashbez 3:247; Behag [1:Hilchot Brachot: 9]; Ravad [Katuv Sham, Berakhot ch. 9]; and

The Rema's general willingness to allow for adaptations of these blessings, in contrast to Rabbi Karo's demand that a convert omit this blessing as inaccurate in its standard wording, probably also lies at the root of the debate between the Shulchan Aruch and Rema in OC 46:6 as regards blessing *hanoten la'ayef koach*. The Shulchan Aruch plainly states that it is inappropriate to bless this blessing, which is not mentioned in the Talmud, while the Rema in his gloss supports the practice:[22]

יש נוהגין לברך: הנותן ליעף כח, ואין דבריהם נראין

Some have the custom to recite the blessing "Who gives strength to the weary", but their words do not appear correct.

הגה: אך המנהג פשוט בבני האשכנזים לאומרה

[Rema's] Gloss: But the normal custom among the Ashkenazim is to say it.

In other words, the medieval Ramah through Rabbi Karo (and the Bach) felt that the wording of a blessing cannot be modified from the Talmudic standard and must be omitted if inaccurate, Rambam felt that the identity blessings do not have to be personally accurate so long as the general point applies to the blesser (and would be fine with the convert blessing *shelo asani goy* along with everybody else since the convert's intent is clear), while Rema – and those who accepted his ruling – felt that identity blessings do not have to be identical in wording for all as long as it is clear that the one who blesses accurately is blessing over the same general point as is everyone else (and so are fine with a convert blessing *she'asani ger/yehudi* since it is the same type of blessing).

C. THE VIEW OF THE MISHNAH BERURAH AND THE ARUCH HASHULCHAN

A careful reading leads one to the conclusion that the Mishna Berurah shares the Rema's position that identity blessings worded differently than in the Talmud are valid as long as they are both accurate and

---

many others.)

22. We recognize that the cases of *sheasani yisrael* and *hanosein layaef koach* are not identical, but our claim is that if the Rema approves of a custom to add a completely new *bracha* unfound in the Talmud, he certainly would have no issue with the change in formulation from *shelo asani goy* to *sheasani yisrael*.

express the underlying idea. Regarding someone who blesses with the formulation of *she'asani yehudi* instead of with the formulation of *shelo asani goy*, Mishnah Berurah (46:16) writes:

ויזהר שלא יברך שעשני ישראל כמו שיש באיזה סדורים ע"י שיבוש הדפום כי י"א
שבזה לא יוכל לברך שוב שלא עשני עבד ולא עשני אשה:

One must be careful not to bless *she'asani yisrael*, the way that it is formulated in some *siddurim* based on a printer's error, since there are those who say that if one does such, one will no longer be allowed to make the blessing "who did not make me a slave" and "who did not make me a woman."

Although the Mishnah Berurah *explicitly* thinks that the positive formulation of *she'asani yisrael* is nothing more than a printer's error,[23] he views the formula as a valid blessing – so much so that the person who blesses thus would have to skip the next two blessings.

In line with this last ruling, Mishna Berurah (46:18) also suggests that a convert should say the Talmudically unsupported version of *she'asani ger*:

... יאמר שעשני גר דמיקרי עשייה כדכתיב ואת הנפש אשר עשו בחרן.

... the convert ought to recite "who made me a convert" since conversion is called making/creating, as it says "the life I made in Charan."

Admittedly, the Mishnah Berurah ends up uncertain whether a convert should actually bless in this fashion; he concludes the paragraph above by quoting the Bach, who questions the whole idea of the blessing *she'asani ger*. However, that doubt is not due to the fact that such a formulation is not found in the Talmud. Rather, it is due to the problem that even this formulation might be false, since it was not God but the convert who made themself Jewish.

Similarly, the Aruch Hashulchan (OC 46:10) is uncertain what to do in light of the Bach's point. He writes:

ואפילו גר בזמן הקדמון היה יכול לברך שני ברכות אלו שלא עשני עבד ושלא
עשני אשה אבל הראשונה אינו יכול לברך שהרי היה כן ויש חולקין גם על שנ(ו)י

---

23. Both the Mishnah Berura and the Aruch Hashulchan seem unaware of the fact that the Shulchan Aruch edition to which the Rema wrote his glosses has the formulation *she'asani yisrael* and that the Rema's gloss – as we discussed – reveals that the Rema certainly did not think it a printer's error.

הברכות [ב"ח] שהרי לא נעשה מבריאתו ישראל אלא שבבחירתו עשה כן ויש
מיישבים זה [ט"ז סק"ז ומג"א סק"י ע"ש]

And even a convert in ancient days was able to bless the two blessings
of *shelo asani eved* and *shelo asani isha*, but the first one [*shelo asani goy*]
one cannot make, because one was created that way. And some [Bach]
also reject the alternative *bracha*[24] because they were not a Jewish person from the time of their creation; rather, through their own choice
they became that. And some (Taz and Magen Avraham) answer this
critique.

Thus, although both the Aruch Hashulchan and the Mishnah Berurah
are uncertain as to how to rule, they accept the basic frameworks of
both the medieval Ramah and the Rema as correct. Both also seem
inclined to follow the view of the Rema in practice.

D. OTHER FORMULATIONS FOUND IN THE *ACHRONIM*

Over time several other formulations and suggestions for dealing
with the issue of the convert's morning blessing have emerged, and
they deserve to be mentioned. First, there are three other formulations, two recent and one ancient, which have been suggested but for
whatever reason have not become part of the accepted canon:

1. *Shehichnisani tachat kanfei haShechina* – "Who brought me in un-
    der the wings of the Divine presence." The Be'er Heiteiv quotes
    Rav Chaim Banvenesti in the Sheyarei Knesset Hagedolah,[25]
    who first proposed this blessing – working under the assumption
    shared with the Rema that the important aspect of an identity
    blessing is to convey thanks for being who you are; the exact

---

24. Our translation of the Aruch Hashulchan corrects what we think is a
typographical error in the standard edition of the Aruch Hashulchan in OC
46:10. The standard edition reading of שני הברכות (two *brachot*), instead of שנוי
הברכות (the changed blessing), simply makes no sense contextually; the Bach does
not rule against a *ger* blessing the other two blessings, but rather only addresses
the alternative (positive) formulation of the first *beracha*. As the new Oz VeHadar
edition of the Aruch Hashulchan with Piskei Mishnah Berura on the bottom
notes simply, if the Aruch Hashulchan is to be understood as referring to the
other two blessings, there is no foundation for that view. That inclines one to
think that this is not his intent. This small textual emendation is evidently what
the Aruch Hashulchan actually intended, as it makes his explanations of the Bach,
Magen Avraham, and Taz all correct.

25. His commentary on the Beit Yosef OC 46.

Talmudic language here is not as important. For a convert, the core meaning of *shelo asani goy* is: Who eventually made me different than all the other Gentiles – i.e., "Who took me in under the wings of the Divine presence." However, this formulation does not escape the problem of inaccuracy pointed out by the Bach – that this is (to the convert's merit) a man-made decision and not an act of God.

2. A more successful formulation is proposed by the Sedei Chemed in the name of the Responsa Zecher Yehosef:[26] *shelo asani goy kigoyei haaratzot* – i.e., "Who did not make me a Gentile like the nations of the land." This formulation is better on a halachic level for two reasons. One: it would be acceptable from the Bach's perspective since it is accurate; it refers to the initial creation, where God made him a Gentile but gave him a different temperament drawn to Judaism.[27] Two: even those who disagreed with the Rema out of concern for changing the Talmudic formulation might have accepted this blessing that keeps the original text intact and merely adds on an additional explanatory phrase after the blessing's words.

3. *Shelo samtani goy* – "Who did not leave me a Gentile." This is actually one of the oldest formulations, appearing in the *siddur* of Rav Saadiah Gaon and in the Cairo Geniza fragments of Seder Tefilah Yashan.[28] This formulation is fine for both someone born Jewish and a convert as it does not touch upon the issue of initial creation at all.

Aside from these three suggestions, there are a number of other suggestions for a convert to deal with this identity blessing.

4. Skip the blessing entirely. This (as noted above) is the opinion of the Bach, and is also the opinion of Rabbi Ovadia Yosef in

---

26. Asafat Dinim 75 quoting Sh"ut Zecher Yehosef Chapter 13. Although the Zecher Yehosef was responding to a quite different question, namely the idea that the Jewish people are also called a "*goy*" (see note 358) and felt that every Jew should make the blessing this way, his position also works well for a convert.

27. Consider the following midrashic tradition related to converts: Bamidbar Rabbah (13:16) as well as BT Shavuot 39a tells us that the souls of all future converts were prepared to be Jews before they even entered into this world.

28. As noted in Rabbi Ari Yitzchak Shvat, "Can a Convert Make the Blessing of 'Who has not made me a Gentile?" Techumin Vol. 15 (1995), p. 444.

Yalkut Yosef.[29] It is problematic for three reasons. On a general level, we do not eliminate blessings when we don't have to do so. Second, in this case particularly, the argument could be made that if the blessing is to thank God for the ability to perform commandments, then a convert, who started life as a Gentile, has even more reason to be thankful than a native-born Jewish person – even more reason to express in some formulation their gratitude for that ability. Third, this suggestion ignores the principle we find in relation to converts in general (and which some count as a positive commandment), that *kachem kager yiheyeh*, we should do all we can to make sure that all Jewish people, no matter their background, partake equally of the practices that are considered important enough to be obligatory.[30]

5. Bless *shelo asani goy* without God's name as suggested by the Kaf Hachaim and the Yaavetz.[31] Ashkenazim might find this solution difficult. Since the Kaf Hachaim and the Yaavetz must feel that the statement "who did not make me a Gentile" is not false (since it would not be okay to utter a falsehood in God's presence even without mentioning His name), the convert might as well bless God explicitly.

6. Bless the standard blessing based on the kabbalist opinion that the creation over which one is blessing is not the initial creation of a person but the recreation that a person experiences every morning upon reawakening.[32] A convert, on the morning after their conversion, and on every ensuing morning, has just as much right to bless *shelo asani goy* as any other Jew.[33]

7. Bless the standard blessing, upon the Taz's opinion that a convert

---

29. Hilchot Hashachar 21. See also the Chidah in Birkei Yosef 46:9 and Maharikash (quoted in Yalkut Yosef OC 46 at p. 33) for others who adopt this view.

30. See Bamidbar 15:15; Shut Ramabam 233; Zet Ra'anan 2:46; and many others.

31. Siddur Beis Yaakov.

32. See Yosef Chaim Eliyahu OD Yosef Chai, commenting on Ben Ish Chai Parshat Vayeishev. Also see Shu"t HaRash 1:191, who implies that these blessings refer to the creation anew every morning.

33. Since the majority of contemporary *poskim* thought that the Avudraham's point was correct, however, we are wary of relying on this view as normative.

is viewed as newborn[34] and can deny to themselves that they, as the person who they are now, was ever previously a Gentile.[35]

Indeed, to the extent that we can see and measure any normative practice, the most common practice we see in our community is that a convert does not make any change in the formulation of this identity blessing – against the view of Rema, Magen Avraham, Taz, Mishnah Berurah, Aruch Hashulchan, and most who have commented on this issue.[36]

E. CONCLUSION

So what is a convert actually supposed to do? We see four choices, each with some flaw. The three initial solutions are clearly problematic, and the final one is valuable only in very unusual Orthodox communities.

1. A convert can recite one of the alternative versions of the blessings discussed in Part D. The problem with this approach is that unusual blessings separate a convert from the rest of the community and that none of these texts have been endorsed by any major halachic authority.
2. A convert can follow the Rema's version in the Darchei Moshe – a view considered acceptable in both the Mishna Berurah and the Aruch Hashulchan – and bless *she'asani ger*. The problem with this solution (besides the Bach's objection to it) is that it is

---

34. BT Yevamot 22a, 97b.

35. Taz (OC 46:5). Since the majority of contemporary *poskim* thought that the Avudraham's point was correct, however, we are wary of relying on this view as normative.

36. Nonetheless, the forthcoming [still not published] new Rabbinical Council of America *siddur* states the following as guidance:

שלא עשני גוי – **Who has not made me a Gentile.** Converts do not make this blessing. Some halachic authorities opine that converts – people who have become Jewish through their own active choice – should omit this blessing altogether, as they weren't made Jewish by any external influence (Avudraham). However, others suggest that a convert should recognize the Divine guidance that led to his choice, and recommend a variety of alternative formulations, such as שהכניסני תחת כנפי השכינה, "Who has brought me under the wings of the Divine Presence" or שעשני גר, "Who has made me into a convert." This matter has not been settled in the halachic literature (Mishnah Berurah), and a *rav* should be consulted.

unwise to encourage a blessing that separates a convert from a born-Jew in matters of liturgy, as the Rambam notes.

3. A convert can adopt the view of the Rambam and make no change in the text of the blessing at all. The problem with this approach is that, according to many, it requires blessing a false blessing – inasmuch as the explanations of the Kabbalists and of the Taz are far from persuasive. Nonetheless, this view seems to be the most common in actual practice.[37]

4. A convert can follow the Rema's ruling in Shulchan Aruch and bless *she'asani yisrael* if the convert is more comfortable blessing via a formulation that all Jews can bless[38] – a valid formulation adopted by such luminaries as the Rosh, Rema, Levush, and Vilna Gaon.[39] However, this formulation in practice still distinguishes between convert and born-Jews in our communities in which no one else blesses God with that version. It is the best option only when others in the community are also blessing *she'asani yisrael*, a rare custom in contemporary (American) Judaism.[40] (Moreover, if a community were to adopt this practice to avoid having converts feel excluded, then we suspect that one must be strict for the view of the Bach, Magen Avraham and Mishnah Berurah and leave out the two remaining identity blessings of *shelo asani eved* and *shelo asani isha*,[41] with all of the complexities that entails.)

Although there are problems with each choice, we do think that the approach of Rav Ovadia Yosef to simply omit this blessing should not be followed in most communities in America, and his approach is in fact not generally cited by Ashkenazi *poskim*.

In any case, a convert leading services clearly should bless the

---

37. However, it is worth noting that Rabbi Mordechai Willig, in conversation with this author, endorses this view based on his desire to not have the convert deviate from the recitations of others as the Rambam notes. This writer also thinks such is a completely reasonable approach.

38. And indeed this may be halachically preferable.

39. For the Rosh, see (at least in some versions) BT Berachot 60b; Rema is explained throughout this article, Levush is at OC 46:5 and Gra is OC 46:4. As an additional proof that this read of the Gra is correct, see Sedai Chemed Maarerchet Cherufin, Asifat dinim 5 s.v. umedi vedri on page 174 in which the Sedai Chemed notes this to be the view of the Gra. See also Yad Chanoch 1 for a more contemporary authority who endorses this version of the *bracha*.

40. See Yad Chanoch (1), who also endorses this change.

41. Bach OC 46:7, Magen Avraham OC 46:9 and Mishnah Berura 46:15. See also Chayei Adam 8:2, who expands on this.

standard formulation used in the community whose prayer he is leading. This is the case for at least three reasons. The first is that the blessings that he blesses in that role are reflective of the entire community and not just of him; as an emissary he can recite that which is true of the general congregation. The second is that there are enough opinions to support a convert blessing with the standard formulation rather than cause any confusion in the communal prayer. The third is that there are enough opinions to support a convert blessing with the standard formulation rather than cause a fellow Jew embarrassment.[42]

---

42. Additional reasons are: (1) Despite the fact that in general we (Ashkenazim) follow the rulings of the Rema, the Be'er Heiteiv does bring down in the name of the Yad Aharon that a convert can make the *bracha* of *shelo asani goy*. In this situation, we can comfortably rely on the Magen Avraham, the Sheyarei Knesset Hagedolah, the Rashaz, the Yaavetz (in the Siddur Beis Yaakov), and the Kaf Hachaim, who all quote this opinion. (2) Even our earliest source explicitly addressing the question, the much-quoted Avudraham, never stated that the convert not saying *shelo asani goy* because of a falsehood was an iron-clad rule; he ended off his opinion with the somewhat ambivalent *vechein hadaat noteh*, "and this seems logical." (3) The Darchei Moshe himself notes that maybe the word *sheasani* doesn't *really* negate the inclusion of a convert, since the convert merited God's assistance in the process of converting, and so God also made the convert the Jew that they became. For all of these reasons, when leading the congregation the convert should recite the communal text of the blessing even if it is *shelo asani goy*. See Igrot Moshe OC 2:29 and many other places for more on why the chazzan should never deviate from the public customs – including the texts – in communal prayer.

(Nor can one claim that modern times are different as we do not fulfill our obligations for *brachot* from the *chazzan*, since SA OC 46:2 makes it clear that one can rely on the services of the *chazzan* by answering "amen" to these blessings. Moreover, Mishnah Berura (46:13) quotes the Magen Avraham in the name of the Levush who rules that the *chazzan* may bless on behalf of even those who know how to pray, provided that there is a *minyan* present.)

May a Convert be a Member
of a Rabbinical Court for Conversion?

Until a century ago, conversions were relatively infrequent and thus did not demand much practical halachic discussion.[1] The increase in converts within the Orthodox community since then, however, has increased related questions of halacha.[2] We must now answer questions that were not discussed explicitly in the past. One such question is related to the blessed phenomenon of converts and their children having become an active part of the Orthodox Jewish community, with many achieving leadership roles – some learning in Yeshiva for decades and becoming rabbis.

As a result of the increased presence of converts within the Jewish community, the following new halachic question has emerged: Is it permissible for a convert to serve as a judge of a *bet din* overseeing a conversion? This is a serious topic since, as is true for any halachic matter that needs a *bet din*, an unacceptable *bet din* can jeopardize the process. This is especially important with regard to conversions due to the serious consequences associated with questionable conversions.

This article addresses that question. Section One of this article discusses the Talmudic sources that pertain to the general qualifications that govern membership of a *bet din*. Section Two considers the medieval *Rishonim* and the Shulchan Aruch's analysis of those Talmudic sources. Section Three surveys the more recent rabbinic discussions that specifically address the acceptability of a convert as a member of a *bet din* that is presiding over a conversion. The Conclusion of this article both summarizes the discussion of whether

---

1. See for example the first footnote in Aruch Hashulchan, Yoreh Deah 268, which makes it clear that conversions were very rare.

2. See for example, Michael Broyde and Shmuel Kadosh, "Book Review: Transforming Identity," *Tradition*, Volume 42:1 Spring 2009 at pages 84–103.

converts can serve on a *bet din* for conversion and includes a recommendation of a normative halachic practice that would be best for all parties involved.

I. THE TALMUD'S DISCUSSION OF A CONVERT SERVING ON A *BET DIN*

Although none of the classical Talmudic sources specifically address the question of whether a convert can serve on a *bet din* that is presiding over a conversion, classical Talmudic sources do address the restrictions and requirements that halacha places on a *dayan* of a rabbinical court. Among the qualifications necessary to judge on a rabbinical court in various types of cases, Mishnah Niddah 6:4 states the general rule that:

כל הראוי לדון דיני נפשות ראוי לדון דיני ממונות, ויש שראוי לדון דיני ממונות ואינו ראוי לדון דיני נפשות. כל הכשר לדון כשר להעיד, ויש שכשר להעיד ואינו כשר לדון.

Anyone who is fit to judge capital cases is fit to judge monetary cases, but there are those who are fit to judge monetary cases that are not fit to judge capital cases. Anyone fit to judge is fit to be a witness, but there are those who are fit to be a witness but are not fit to judge.

This source tells us that depending on the subject matter of the case, the requirements for *dayanim* vary. There are four possible tiers of "fitness": (1) those who are fit to judge capital cases, monetary cases, and to be a witness; (2) those who are fit to judge [monetary cases] and to be a witness; (3) those who are fit only to be a witness; (4) those who are fit neither to judge nor to testify. From this source we can gather that more serious matters have stricter requirements. For example, capital cases are more serious than are commercial cases and the Mishnah has stricter requirements for capital cases.

Mishnah Sanhedrin (4:2) spells out who is fit to judge capital cases, and from this information implies who is fit to judge financial cases. It states:

דיני הטומאות והטהרות מתחילין מן הגדול דיני נפשות מתחילין מן הצד הכל כשרין לדון דיני ממונות ואין הכל כשרין לדון דיני נפשות אלא כהנים לוים וישראלים המשיאין לכהונה:

Anyone is fit to judge a monetary case, but not everyone is fit to judge a capital case; only Kohens, Levites, and Israelites who can marry into a Kohen's family.

According to this mishnah, Jewish men who if they had been women would have been ineligible to marry a Kohen, are unfit to judge capital cases. The Mishnah reasons that the more authority one person can exercise over another, the more that person ought to be a natural member of society. An indication in Jewish law of a person being a "natural" member of Jewish society is one's acceptability to marry into all families, including those of Kohanim.

This type of distinction is standard for a legal system. Many legal systems similarly restrict access to high political office to people who are natural born citizens. For example, the U.S. Constitution states in article II, Clause 1 that:

> No person except a natural born Citizen, or a Citizen of the United States, at the time of the Adoption of this Constitution, shall be eligible to the Office of President.

If one became an American citizen through "conversion" ("naturalization"), he or she cannot become the President (or the Vice President)[3] of the United States. This is analogous to the Jewish law that a convert cannot become a king of the Jewish people[4] or even a judge of capital cases (above).

This demand, that only fully integrated natural members of society can be qualified to serve as judges, does not apply to monetary cases. A *berraita* quoted in Yerushalmi Sanhedrin[5] tells us explicitly

---

3. Inferred from the Twelfth Amendment to the United States Constitution which states that: "[N]o person constitutionally ineligible to the office of President shall be eligible to that of Vice-President of the United States."

The historical source for the American law rule is uncertain. Alexander Heard and Michael Nelson in *Presidential Selection*, page 123 (Duke University Press, 1987) seem to indicate that one possible source of the natural born citizen clause can be traced to a letter of July 25, 1787, from John Jay (who was born in New York) to George Washington (who was born in Virginia), presiding officer of the Constitutional Convention. John Jay wrote: "Permit me to hint, whether it would be wise and seasonable to provide a strong check to the admission of Foreigners into the administration of our national Government; and to declare expressly that the Commander in Chief of the American army shall not be given to nor devolve on, any but a natural born Citizen." There was no debate, and this qualification for the office of the Presidency was introduced by the drafting Committee, and then adopted without discussion by the Constitutional Convention. (See also the Wikipedia entry for "Natural born citizen of the United States.")

4. See Rambam Laws of Kings 1:4.

5. Tractate Sanhedrin 4:8.

that "anyone is fit to judge a monetary case." Rabbi Yehuda explains: "Even a *mamzer*."[6] Rabbi Yehuda uses the term "even" because a *mamzer* is not only barred from marrying into a Kohen's family; they are also barred from marrying into any Israelite family. Yet, the *berraita* permits the *mamzer* to serve on a *bet din* judging financial matters. Bavli Sanhedrin[7] points out that this allowance applies to converts, too:

הכל כשרין לדון דיני ממונות. הכל לאתויי מai? אמר רב יהודה: לאתויי ממזר.
הא תנינא חדא זימנא:
כל הראוי לדון דיני נפשות - ראוי לדון דיני ממונות, ויש ראוי לדון דיני ממונות
ואין ראוי לדון דיני נפשות. והוינן בה: לאתויי מ‎אי? ואמר רב יהודה: לאתויי ממזר!
חדא לאתויי גר, וחדא לאתויי ממזר.
וצריכא: דאי אשמעינן גר - דראוי לבא בקהל, אבל ממזר - אימא לא. ואי
אשמעינן ממזר - דבא מטיפה כשרה, אבל גר דלא בא מטיפה כשרה - אימא לא,
צריכא.

"Anyone is fit to judge a monetary case" – who does the word "anyone" include? Rabbi Yehuda said: "It comes to include a *mamzer*."

Wasn't this already taught?

"Anyone who is fit to judge capital cases can judge monetary cases, but not everyone who is fit to judge monetary cases is fit to judge capital cases." The question was asked: "Who does [the word] 'anyone' include? And Rabbi Yehuda said: "It comes to include a *mamzer*!"

One of the [mishnayot] comes to include a *mamzer* and one of them comes to include a convert.

And this is necessary, for if it told us [only] about a convert, we might assume that this is because the convert is fit to 'enter the community' [i.e., to marry into most families] but we would have said no as regards a *mamzer*. And if it told to us [only] about a *mamzer*, we might assume this is because the *mamzer* came from Jewish parents, but we would have said no as regards a convert – who did not come from Jewish parents. Hence they are both necessary to teach that both [a *mamzer* and a convert] may serve on a *bet din*.

Serving on a *bet din* for a financial matter is fundamentally different than serving as a judge on a capital case.

---

6. A *mamzer* is a child resulting from a sexual relationship between two Jewish people ineligible to marry each other at the moment of conception. A *mamzer* is precluded from marrying Kohanim, Leviim, and Israelites.

7. Sanhedrin 36b.

One obvious rationale for this distinction is that the parties of a commercial dispute are free to choose the judges or solitary judge to rule on their case.[8] Since in financial cases a mere monetary asset or interest is in dispute and since individuals have complete ownership and authority over their monetary assets, disputants can accept whatever judges they wish.[9] This is in stark contrast to capital cases where the accused are not free to craft a court that is to their liking.[10] This lack of free choice is not merely due to the imposition of state force against a defendant. Rather, Jewish Law does not allow a party to agree to be executed.[11] In contrast to financial interests, individuals do not have complete ownership and dominion over their bodies[12] and capital cases entail the highest level of adjudication in Jewish law. Halacha thus reserves the authority to impose death to those Jews who, among other qualifications, are trusted cultural insiders.

This reasoning is implied by Rava in Bavli Yevamot,[13] where he also spells out a more restrictive view for a *bet din* that presides over a *chalitza* release of a widow from levirate ties to her deceased husband's brothers:

תני רב שמואל בר יהודה:

"בישראל" - בב"ד של ישראל ולא בב"ד של גרים. . . .

אמר רבא: גר דן את חבירו דבר תורה, שנאמר: "שום תשים עליך מלך אשר יבחר ה' אלהיך בו מקרב אחיך תשים עליך מלך", עליך הוא דבעינן מקרב אחיך, אבל גר דן את חבירו גר; ואם היתה אמו מישראל - דן אפי' ישראל. ולענין חליצה - עד שיהא אביו ואמו מישראל, שנאמר: ונקרא שמו בישראל.

Rabbi Shmuel bar Yehuda taught over a *berraita*:

"[And the name of (the one who releases his childless brother's widow) shall be called] in Israel [the house of the removed shoe]" (Deuteronomy 25:10) – through a *bet din* of born-Jews and not through a *bet din* of converts. . . .

---

8. See Shulchan Aruch, Choshen Mishpat 3:1.

9. This includes a person who gives money to somebody who is not as a matter of Jewish law entitled to it.

10. In the Jewish tradition a person is not even the owner of their own body and thus cannot agree to have themselves killed, and certainly may not commit suicide.

11. To explain this, consider the following: if a person confesses to owing another person money, their statement is adequate to enforce them to pay the money, whereas if one confesses to a capital crime, one cannot be executed based on that confession.

12. Suicide, for example, is thus prohibited; see for example Yoreh Deah 345:1.

13. Yevamot 101b–102a.

Rava states that a convert may judge their fellow convert as a matter of Torah law as it states "Ye shall place upon you a King chosen by God. From among your brothers ye shall choose a king over yourselves. "Over ye" requires "from among your brothers," but a convert may judge a fellow convert. If one's mother is Jewish, the convert can judge even a [born] Jew. But for *chalitza*, both mother and father must be Jewish – as it says "and his name shall be called in Israel" (Deuteronomy 25:10).

The very nature of *chalitza* as an event of changed status effected through public recognition requires that the presiding *dayanim* meet even stricter insider lineage requirements. Thus, a Jew who is a convert, or even the child of a convert, is ineligible to serve on the *bet din* – regardless of whether the widow being released is a convert herself and whether the releasing man and his deceased brother were born to parents who had converted. Unlike financial matters wherein Rava ruled that a convert may impose judgment on a convert, this judicial officiation changes the woman's status by validating the widow's release from levirate marriage requires Jewish officiants of born Jewish parentage.[14]

II. *RISHONIM* AND SHULCHAN ARUCH ON CONVERTS IN A *BET DIN*

The *Rishonim* and the Shulchan Aruch glean from these Talmudic sources a number of rules regarding the acceptability of converts.[15]
The Rambam writes:

בית דין של שלשה שהיה אחד מהן גר הרי זה פסול, עד שתהיה אמו מישראל ...[16].
הכל כשרים לדון דיני ממונות אפילו גר והוא שתהיה אמו מישראל.
וגר דן את חבירו הגר אף על פי שאין אמו מישראל ...[17].
והחליצה ... בפני שלשה שיודעין להקרות ... ואם היה אחד מן השלשה גר,
פסול. ...

---

14. As Rabbi Shalom Yosef Elyashiv notes (as cited in the next section).

15. For clarity's sake, it is necessary to note a linguistic peculiarity found in the sources. In the time of the Talmud, *Rishonim*, and Shulchan Aruch the word *ger* was often used to denote either a non-Jew who converted to Judaism or the child of a convert. Thus while we might find the phrase "a *ger* whose mother converted" to be an oxymoron, this phrase is used repeatedly in the classical, pre-modern sources.

16. MT Sanhedrin 2:9.

17. MT Sanhedrin 11:11.

ואפילו היה אביו גר ואמו ישראלית, לא תחלוץ עד שיהיה אביו ואמו מישראל.[18]

An [appointed[19]] *bet din* of three [i.e., a local court of judicial corpo-
ral punishment and of penalties and fines], one of whom is a convert
whose mother is not a born-Jewess, is an invalid *bet din* . . .

All are valid to [be appointed to[20]] judge monetary matters, even a
convert – as long as his mother is a born-Jewess.

A convert whose mother is not Jewish [i.e., an actual convert], may
judge his fellow convert [in monetary matters]. . . .

Release from levirate marriage . . . is in front of three who know
how to read aloud . . . and is invalid if one of the three is a convert.
Even if [only] his father is a convert and his mother is a born-Jewess
instead of both his father and mother being born-Jews, [the woman]
should not be released.

According to the Rambam, an actual convert[21] may preside over converts alone and only in financial disputes between converts.

The Shulchan Aruch writes similarly:

לענין דין: גר כשר לדון דיני ממונות, והוא שתהא אמו מישראל. אבל אם אין אמו
מישראל, פסול לדון את ישראל אבל לחבירו גר דן. ולחליצה פסול, אפילו לחליצת
גרים, עד שיהא אביו ואמו מישראל. [22] . . .

בית דין של ג' שהיה אחד מהם גר, הרי זה פסול לדון לישראל אלא אם כן היתה
אמו מישראל. וגר דן את חבירו הגר אף על פי שאין אמו מישראל.[23] . . .

מצות חליצה בג' דיינים ישראלים. . . . נמצא אחד מהם . . . גר, פסול – ואפילו
היה אביו גר ואמו ישראלית, פסול עד שיהא אביו ואמו מישראל.[24]

As regards judging: A convert is valid to judge monetary matters as
long as his mother is a born-Jewess. If his mother is not a born-Jewess,
he is not allowed to judge a Jew but may judge a fellow convert. For release from levirate marriage [however], he is invalid unless his mother
and father are born-Jews – even for release from levirate marriages
that involves converts [such as when the widow is a convert or as when
the deceased and his brother are the sons of converts]. . . .

A court of three in which one member is a convert whose mother

---

18. MT Levirate Marriage and Release 4:5.

19. On the court being an appointed court see MT Sanhedrin 2:8.

20. On the judge being an appointed judge see MT Sanhedrin 2:8.

21. Meaning the person who actually converted to Judaism, but not his
children.

22. ShA Yoreh Deah 269:11.

23. ShA Chosen Mishpat 7:1.

24. Even HaEzer 169:1–2.

is not a born-Jewess, is invalid to judge born-Jews. But a convert may judge his fellow convert, even if his mother is not a born-Jewess. . . .

The mitzva of release from levirate marriage is through three Jewish judges. . . . If one of them is found to be . . . a convert, it is invalid. Even if [only] his father is a convert and his mother a born-Jewess, it is invalid; [both] his father and his mother have to be born-Jews.

According to the Shulchan Aruch, too, an actual convert may preside over converts alone and only in financial disputes between converts. All subsequent restatements of Jewish law have accepted these rules that limit converts to judging only converts and only in monetary matters – or to judging born-Jews in monetary matters but only by the consent of the parties.[25] Medieval *Rishonim* did debate whether the son of a convert mother and a born-Jew may also judge born-Jews in monetary matters[26] and may also preside over the release of a levirate marriage.[27] Even as regards an actual convert, we do have an anomalous ruling by Rashi that permits him to judge fellow converts in capital cases, too – as long as the convert on trial agrees to accept the convert as a judge.[28] However, all authorities agree that a convert is prohibited from presiding at a release from levirate marriage and that even the son of converts (if both the parents are converts) may not sit as such a *dayan*. All agree that an actual convert may not judge a born-Jew against their will, even as regards financial matters. And as regards Rashi's position of allowing a convert to judge another convert with the latter's consent in a tribunal for a capital case: not only Rambam's legal predecessor, the Rif, [29] but also Tosafot,[30] through the Rosh[31] to the Tur[32] accept the Rambam and Shulchan Aruch position that limits a convert to judging a convert in financial matters alone.

In sum, as regards the types of judgments that we have discussed, an actual convert may sit as a judge only for financial cases and only if all parties to the case are converts or consensually accept him as

---

25. See Aruch Hashulchan CM 7:1–5, as well as Kovetz HaPoskim on Chosen Mishpat 7:1.
26. For example, see Rema Chosen Mishpat 7:1 in the name of the Tosafot.
27. For example, see Rema Even HaEzer 169:2 in the name of the SeMaG.
28. Rashi, Yevamot 102a, s.v. *ger dan cheveor ger.*
29. Rif, Sanhedrin 13b.
30. Tosafot, Yevamot 102a s.v. *ger.*
31. Rosh, Sanhedrin 3:10.
32. Tur, Yoreh Deah 269.

a judge. The one area of judgment that is still unclear is whether a convert may sit as a *dayan* on a conversion panel.

III. MAY A CONVERT SERVE ON A *BET DIN* FOR A CONVERSION?

To the best of my knowledge, there is no discussion in the pre-modern sources as to whether a convert may sit on a *bet din* for conversions. Rather, the first authority to address this issue is Rabbi Shlomo Kluger (1783–1869). In his notes on Shulchan Aruch Even HaEzer[33] he states:

... גוף הדין אם גר כשר להיות ב"ד לקבל גרים, אין זה ברור. הנה הן אמת לדעת
רש"י יבמות ק"ב (ע"א ד"ה גר) דגר דן את חברו גר הוי אפילו לדיני נפשות, פשיטא
דיכול לקבל גרים ג"כ. אך לדעת התוס' (ד"ה גר) החולקים שם וס"ל דדיני נפשות
אינו יכול לדון, ובע"כ היכי דבעינן מומחים לא מהני גר אפילו לחברו גר. וא"כ הרי
התוס' ביבמות דף מו' (ע"ב ד"ה משפט) כתבו דגרות דומה לגזלות וחבלות דבעינן
דוקא ג' ומומחים ומה שמקבלים גרים בזמן הזה הוי רק מכח שליחותייהו דקמאי
עבדינן, וא"כ י"ל היינו רק ישראלים הראוים להיות מומחים אז הוי שליחותייהו
דקמאי ... אבל גר דאינו ראוי להיות מומחה ... י"ל דאינו בר שליחות. ... ולכן
לדעת התוס' נראה דגר אסור לקבל גרים.

... As to whether a convert can be [on] a *bet din* to accept converts, the matter is unclear. It is true that according to Rashi in Yevamot 102a (s.v. *ger*), [who understands] that a convert's fitness to judge his fellow convert even applies to capital matters, it is obvious that he can [sit on a *bet din* to] accept converts as well. But according to Tosafot (idem, s.v. *ger*) who disagree and opine that he cannot judge capital matters, a convert is not valid [to judge] even a fellow convert in matters that require expert judges. Ergo, since Tosafot Yevamot 46b (s.v. *mishpat*) wrote that conversion is similar to robbery and assault in requiring expert judges and that we accept converts today [without expert judges] only because we carry out the commission of the early generations, only Jews who are fit to be expert judges can fulfill the commission ... but a convert, as one who is not fit to be an expert judge ... is not fit to fulfill this commission. ... Thus, it appears that according to Tosafot's view a convert is forbidden to [sit on a *bet din* to] accept converts.

Rabbi Kluger contends that conversion is similar to more serious communal issues of robbery and violence rather than to mere monetary disputes and, thus, requires the same higher standards for a

---

33. Published in his Responsa Tuv Tam Vedat, volume 6, page 595.

rabbinical court.[34] Since normative halacha follows the majority view expressed in Tosafot that excludes converts from serving on capital cases even for converts,[35] Rabbi Kluger posits that the majority view also excludes a convert from presiding over any type of case that would theoretically require expert law judges, including conversions.

Responsa Bemareh Habazak, a multi-volume collection of questions and short answers with annotations prepared by the Israeli Eretz Hemdah Institute under the leadership of Rabbi Shaul Yisraeli (1910–1995), accepts Rabbi Kluger's logic.[36] However, Rabbi Yisraeli adds that a conversion in which a convert sat on the *bet din* is valid *de facto* based on the possibility either that Rashi might be correct that a convert may judge converts in capital cases[37] and similarly in any case requiring expert law judges, or that the view that a conversion is valid with just one *dayan* rather than three[38] might be correct – so that the solitary convert judge on a panel is not critical to a conversion.[39] Similarly, the Responsa Bet Mordechai 1:81, the Aderet's Maneh Eliyahu 8, and Dayan Grossnass in Lev Aryeh 21 accept such a conversion as minimally valid.

In North America, Rabbi Gedalya Felder (1921–1991)[40] rejected Rabbi Kluger's argument that judging conversion is similar to judg-

---

34. This comparison is probably based on the understanding that one problematic issue of a convert serving as a judge is the concern over *serara* (power and authority) – a concern spelled out explicitly by Rabbi Akiva Eiger (gloss on ShA Yoreh Deah 269:1) – which is more problematic as regards conversion than as regards reimbursable monetary matters.

35. See Tur Yoreh Deah 268.

36. Bemarah Habazak 3:82 (at page 136). (This volume is the last one where every *teshuva* published was approved by Rav Shaul Yisraeli.)

37. A small group of *Rishonim* adopt Rashi's view that a *ger* can sit on death penalty cases involving a convert (see Bach on Choshen Mishpat 7 who cites Rabbenu Yerucham as adopting Rashi's view).

38. Mordechai in Yevamot 36 cites the view of Rabbi Yehuda ben Yom Tov and Rabbenu Simcha that conversion needs but a single *dayan*, and Tosafot (Kiddushin 62b s.v. ger) ponders such a possibility, albeit concluding that such is not to be followed *lehalacha*. Nearly all the *Rishonim* accept Tosafot's view.

39. I find this view that such a conversion is valid *bede'eved* based on these two factors is beyond my ability to fully understand, as both Rashi's view and the view that a conversion is valid with just one *dayan* are rejected *lehalacha* by the Shulchan Aruch and by almost everyone else.

40. Nachalat Tzvi 1:226–227; note, this *teshuva* is only found in the second edition of this work and not the first. See also Rabbi Chanoch Henoch Cohen, *"Be-inyan Ger ha'im mutar letzorfo l'dayan Bebeit Din shel shelosha be-kabbalat Ger"* Shanah beShanah 5752 259–265.

ing capital matters. Rabbi Felder rules that conversion is most similar to a financial court case. Therefore, the postulant who becomes a convert can accept a convert judge to effect the conversion, just as a convert can accept a convert judge for financial matters:

...גר...ראוי...לקבל גרים....היות: דקיי"ל דגר דן את חברו גר (יבמות ק"ב ע"א)
...וכן אפסק בשו"ע (יו"ד רס"ט י"א, חו"מ ז א) דבדיני ממונות דן את חברו גר, וגרות
הלא משפט כתיב בי' ומזה ידעינן דבעינן שלשה (יבמות מ"ו ע"ב), לא שונה גירות
דיני ממונות. וכן מצאתי בעיוני בדבר, בשו"ת שארית ישראל להגאון ר' ישראל
זאב מינצבערג ז"ל (יו"ד סי' כ"ב) שדן בזה בקיצור והעלה להתיר שב"ד של גרים
יקבלו גרים ולטפל בכל ענייני הגירות. . . .
מיהו . . . הנהו אינשי דלא מעלי – שאינם שומרי מצוות – אין ממש במעשיהם,
דמה דאין לו אינו יכול להקנות לאחרים . . .

... A convert ... is fit ... to accept converts. ... Inasmuch as it is established that a judge can judge his fellow convert (Yevamot 102a) ... as Shulchan Aruch (Yoreh Deah 269:11; Choshen Mishpat 7:1) rules that a convert can judge other converts in financial matters and inasmuch as conversion is referred to Biblically as "judgment"[41] from which we know that three judges are needed (Yevamot 46b), conversion is no different than financial judgments [as regards the fitness of a convert to judge a convert]. When looking into the matter, I found that the great Rabbi Israel Zev Mintzberg in Responsa She'erit Yisrael (Yoreh Deah 22) dealt with this matter concisely and ruled permissively that a court of converts may accept converts and be involved in every matter related to conversion. . . .

However ... the [converting] actions of [born] Jews who are unsuitable – who do not observe the commandments – are meaningless. After all, one cannot grant another that which he himself does not have . . .

As a reasonable proof to this view, one could add the following: in explaining why a conversion that began during the day may be completed at night if necessary, the Taz (Yoreh Deah 268:9) compares a rabbinical court supervising conversions to a rabbinical court judging financial matters.

Rabbi Kluger's ruling invalidating a convert as a conversion judge, however, also continued to be maintained. Rabbi Shalom

---

41. The reference is to Numbers 15:16 or Deuteronomy 1:16 as discussed in Yevamot 46b.

Yosef Elyashiv (b. 1910) negated the relevance of discussing whether conversion is more similar to robberies and assaults or more similar to mere monetary matters. In a printed collection of his lectures as recorded by his students,[42] he points out that the *dayanim* judging conversion are not judging the convert alone as much as they are judging between the postulant, on the one hand, and the Jewish people who accepts converts, on the other hand. Thus, inasmuch as a convert cannot impose judgment on born-Jews even in monetary matters, a convert cannot judge a conversion:

כתבו התוס' בכתובות (מ"ד ע"ב ד"ה ואימא) דהגם דגר פסול להיות דיין מ"מ גר יכול לדון את הגרים. והכי קיי"ל:16.

אכן נראה דלעניין לגייר את הגרים (דבעינן בפני שלשה) אז פסול דיין שהוא גר, ומשום דעצם קבלת הגרים זה נחשב שדן את ישראל, דהרי זהו נדון להכניס גרים אל קהל ה', ונחשב שדן בזה את כללות קהל ה', וזה נחשב שדן את ישראל. כן נראה פשוט בסברא.

Tosafot in Ketubot (44b s.v. veama) write that although a convert cannot be a judge [for born-Jews], he can judge converts. This is the halacha.

From this it appears that for matters of conversion (which require three [judges]) a convert *dayan* is invalid since accepting converts is itself a form of judging Jews; since the judgment is about bringing converts into the congregation of God, the Jewish community, [t]he [judge] is judging the congregation of God as a group and that means that he is judging [born] Jews. This seems obvious.

The editor of the volume[43] then adds:

(ושאלתי את רבינו אם זה מעכב את הגירות כשאחד הדיינים היה גר, ואמר רבינו שלדעתו זה לעיכובא.)

(And I asked our Rabbi [Elyashiv] if one of the *dayanim* having been a convert voids the conversion even after the fact, and he said that in his view it does.)

In a decision issued by the rabbinical court in Jerusalem over a decade ago to invalidate a convert judge of conversions, this leading court has reframed the question even further than does Rabbi Elyashiv's

---

42. See Rabbi Shalom Yosef Elyashiv, *He'arot BeMasechet Kiddushin* page 436.
43. Or the student who wrote down the lecture.

opinion.[44] The court concluded that conversions and *chalitza* release
from levirate marriage are similar in that they are both changes in the
halachic status of the person. Therefore, the standards for a rabbinical court are the same for both. This view suggests that regardless
of when a convert may serve on a *bet din* in general, members of a
bet din for a conversion or for *chalitza* serve as the gatekeepers of an
individual's new halachic status, and this role is inappropriate for a
convert. Rabbi Hershel Schachter indicates a preference for this view
as well.[45]

To summarize, we have discussed five views that can be divided
into two groups. One group permits or at least validates a conversion
in which one of the judges was a convert and the other group invali-
dates such conversion:

In the first group: (1) Rabbi Felder argues to validate a convert
judge accepted by a postulant because conversion is merely an act of
court validating the reality that a person has adopted Judaism – similar to a court judging simple financial matters. (2) Rabbi Yisraeli is
stricter in accepting the view that evaluating conversion is more comparable in weight to evaluating robberies and assaults. Accordingly,
he does forbid converts to sit as conversion judges. Nonetheless, he
accepts *de facto* a conversion through a court on which a convert sat
– on the grounds both that it is a serious judgment of a convert alone
and that the convert was also accepted by a born-Jew *dayan* as one of
the panel members. Such *de facto* acceptance of a conversion in which
a convert served as one of the judges is also adopted by many other
rabbinic authorities.

In the second group: (3) Rabbi Kluger, in the earliest ruling on
the topic, argued that judging conversion is comparable in weight to
the serious judgment of robbery and assault. Due to the weightiness
of conversion, he forbids conversions through a panel that includes
a convert judge (but acknowledges that there is a rejected minority
view that would allow a convert to judge conversions). (4) Rabbi
Elyashiv argues that even if conversion is not so weighty an issue
and is more similar to financial matters, a conversion through even
one convert judge is invalid since it is a judgment that affects the
Jewish people and not merely the convert. (5) The rabbinical court

---

44. See Dinei Mamonot u-Berurai Yuchasin 7:416.
45. See Rabbi Hershel Schachter, *"Bedin Ger Dan Chavero Ger"* Kol Zvi 5762
294–301 at page 299. Rabbi Schachter quotes this view in the name of Rabbi
Shmuel Lev Yulov, Shalmei Shmuel 45.

of Jerusalem and Rabbi Hershel Schachter argue that the relevant issue is the judgment of status. Just as is true regarding *chalitza*, only born-Jews can grant any new status.

IV. CONCLUSION AND DETERMINING THE NORMATIVE HALACHIC PRACTICE

The basis of this dispute can perhaps be found in the Shach's pondering of two competing understandings of the nature of conversions. In explaining the ruling codified in the Shulchan Aruch that a convert can accept the commandments only during the day even as the immersion can be performed at night if necessary, the Shach compares conversion both to monetary cases and to *chalitza* release from levirate marriage. The Shulchan Aruch[46] reads as follows:

כל ענייני הגר, בין להודיעו המצות לקבלם בין המילה בין הטבילה, צריך שיהיו בג' הכשרים לדון, וביום. מיהו דוקא לכתחלה, אבל בדיעבד אם לא מל או טבל אלא בפני ב' ובלילה . . . הוי גר ומותר בישראלית – חוץ מקבלת המצות שמעכבת אם אינה ביום ובשלשה.

All the steps for the convert – whether informing him of the mitzvot so that he might accept them, circumcision, or immersion – must be in front of three who are kosher to judge and during the day. However, that is only an initial requirement; if *de facto* he had circumcised or immersed before only two and at night . . . he is a convert [without qualms] and permitted to [marry] a Jewess. But acceptance of the mitzvot is not valid *de facto* unless it is before three during the day.

The Shach[47] elaborates:

. . . דקבלת מצות הוי כתחילת דין שנתבאר בח"מ סי' ה', אבל טבילה ומילה הוי כגמר דין שנתבאר שם דגומרין בלילה.
וצ"ע קצת דהא כתב הרב שם סעיף ב' די"א אם עברו ודנו בלילה דיניהם דין. אם כן לפ"ז ודאי דאפילו בקבלת מצות סגי בדיעבד בלילה ולא ה"ל להרב למיסתם סתומי.
ואפשר דדוקא לענין דיני ממונות חשש הרב לסברת ההי"א משום דהפקר ב"ד הפקר וכו"כ הב"ח בח"מ סי' ה' דאף על גב דלגבי חליצה יש לפסוק לחומרא דאפילו דיעבד החליצה פסולה בלילה מ"מ כדאי הן הי"א לסמוך עליהם עכ"ל וה"ה הכא דכחליצה דמי:

---

46. ShA Yoreh Deah 268:3.
47. Yoreh Deah 268:9.

... because acceptance of commandments is equivalent to opening a
court case, [which as] discussed in Choshen Mishpat Chapter 5 [must
be during the day], while immersion and circumcision are equivalent
the conclusion of a court case that, as explained there, can be concluded at night.

[However] this ruling is a bit difficult since the Rema wrote in Choshen
Mishpat 5:2 that there are those who say that if a court proceeds and
judges at night its judgment is valid. That being the case, such an approach certainly validates *de facto* an acceptance of commandments at
night, and the Rema should not have been silent here.

A possible answer is that only as regards money matters did the Rema
contemplate that view, inasmuch as a court can freely transfer property. Bach in Choshen Mishpat 5 did state that although as regards
chalitza we must be strict and invalidate a *chalitza* that was done at
night, as regards money matters we rely on the alternative view. The
same [strict] ruling applies here [in conversion] since it is similar to
chalitza [Id.].

In other words: even without the question of a convert serving as a
conversion judge, the Shach saw good reason to view a conversion
both as similar to a mere monetary judgment of verifying ownership
of monies (in that it merely verifies an already committed postulant
as a convert) and as similar to a more serious release of a woman
from levirate ties (through a court of born cultural insiders, in that it
changes the status of a person from Gentile to Jewish).

Inasmuch as there is no precedent source that can clearly resolve
this dispute – which it seems from the Shach is an inherent tension –
it is certainly wise to err on the side of caution and mandate that only
born-Jews serve as *dayanim* in cases of conversion. This is especially
so in light of the fact that there are eminent *poskim* who consider such
conversions invalid even after the fact. It would be a disservice to any
potential convert (as well as to the Jewish community) to intention-
ally staff a conversion panel with a convert judge when there is an
abundance of competent and technically qualified rabbis available.[48]

To explain more fully the halachic rationale behind being strict
on a practical level (in all but the rarest cases): In many matters of
Jewish law, such as whether a particular piece of meat is kosher, the
response to a halachic question that cannot be resolved is for each *bet
din* to follow its own regular *poskim* (*aseh lecha rav*). The problem with

---

48. This point was already made by Rabbi Kluger (above).

adopting this approach as regards conversion is that there are more significant and more long-term consequences. Those who are lenient on this matter produce converts who are still Gentiles according to those who are strict. Consider, for example, a hypothetical *bet din* for conversion staffed exclusively by students of Rabbi Felder. Rabbi Felder certainly was an eminent and respected *posek*. If they follow the rule of *aseh lecha rav*, this *bet din* ought to permit converts to sit on such a conversion panel because that is Rabbi Felder's reasonable understanding of the halacha. Yet, if this hypothetical *bet din* in fact converts in that way, they know full well that another hypothetical *bet din* staffed by students of Rabbi Elyashiv (who also was an eminent *posek*) would consider the people it converted to be Gentiles and the women and children among them to be Gentiles. This result is bad both for the general Jewish community and for the convert at hand.[49]

To state this differently: in terms of the traditional norms for how a court reaches a halachic decision, conversion is similar to divorce. A *bet din* strives as a matter of normative practice to issue *gittin* that are valid according to all views. Only in cases where a *get* cannot be issued consistent with such a standard is any lower standard employed.[50] Similarly, a *bet din* for conversion should only consist of individuals that are valid *dayanim* according to the strictest halachic interpretation unless no other valid *dayanim* are present and a conversion has to be performed (a very rare case). If the *bet din* relies on the strictest rules when there is no reason not to, they can be sure that the *gittin* and conversions that they preside over will be valid and

---

49. I would make the following claim: Even Rabbi Felder, himself, once he is aware of Rabbi Elyashiv's strict view, ought to say *halacha lemaseh*, not to do such a conversion with a convert sitting on the panel, absent a special situation where that was the best that could be done in a special case. Not because Rabbi Felder doubts his own rule, but because it is not wise to put a convert in a situation where others doubt the validity of his or her conversion.

50. See Rivash 399 and Yabia Omer, Even HaEzer 6:6(3); see also Taz, Even HaEzer 17:15, who notes that in time of urgent need (such as a case of *igun*) the consensus rule is not followed. That ought to be exactly the model here. Precisely because there are virtually no cases where only a convert can sit on a panel for conversion, such ought to never happen, just as a *get* that any significant group of *poskim* thinks is invalid need never be given (other than in cases where that is the only way to give the *get*). [Of course, if there were a case where a conversion needed to be done because of some urgent and unexpected *shaat hadechak* and the only panel available included a *ger*, then those who rule such to be permitted are almost obligated to so act – but such cases are very rare in conversions.]

respected within the entire Jewish community as opposed to only being accepted within a smaller segment of the population.

If one, unfortunately, has converted through a panel of *dayanim* that included a convert, the proper policy is to treat this conversion as a *bedi'avad* matter.[51] That means that we should respond to this scenario in two ways. First: since most *poskim* validate such conversion *de facto*, we ought to accept that the conversion is valid and the person Jewish.[52] Second: since there is a strain of thought held by Torah giants over centuries that this conversion is in fact invalid, it is proper that this convert should reaccept the commandments in front of an unquestionably valid rabbinical court and re-immerse in a *mikva* so as to eliminate any such doubt – at least if they have not yet married and have not yet had children.[53] Converts and the Jewish community as a whole are ill-served by having a conversion that others will not accept when with no significant effort they can have a conversion accepted by all.

May we be blessed to live in a time where all conversions are for the sake of heaven and all conversions are handled by conversion panels that are qualified to do so.

---

51. Such a mistake might happen because the *dayanim* involved did not know the halacha, or knew only one side of a complex dispute, or because they did not know that one of the *dayanim* was a *ger*. Of course, it almost goes without saying that measures should be taken to ensure that the mistake is not repeated.

52. Aside from the authorities listed above, consider how the Shulchan Aruch and Tur both note that *chalitza* performed before a *bet din* that included a convert is invalid even *de facto*, while neither source rules similarly as regards conversion. This might indicate that neither the Tur nor the Shulchan Aruch thought that a convert serving as a *dayan* was *pasul* for conversion matters, at least *bedi'avad*.

53. Great thought needs to be put into whether the same advice should be given if the person is a woman and she had already married and had children.

The Children of Two Converts:
Are They Considered *Gerim*?

Introduction

This short note discusses who is considered a *ger* that Jewish law considers worthy of special protections. It first does so by examining whether and which marriage restrictions or marriage leniencies of low status might be demanded of, or allowed to, the children of a convert. It closes with an argument that this way of examining the question might not be very relevant and that special protections and special requirements to love might apply regardless of official status.

Marriage between a Convert and a *Mamzer/et*

There is a fundamental dispute between *Rishonim* about the status of "second generation" (children of) converts. There are two very different ways of thinking about the place of children of converts in the Jewish community. The Rambam maintains that the status of a *ger* is limited to the one who actually converted to Judaism. Everyone else is an Israelite. According to the Rambam, someone who did not convert at any stage, someone whose parents converted before his or her conception, is born into the Jewish people – is a born-Jew. Tosafot understands the status of a *ger* in a fundamentally different way. Tosafot understands that converts along with their progeny form a community of *gerim*, which exists alongside the communities of priests, Levites, and Israelites; converts and their descendants who have not intermarried with born-Jews – including also the son or daughter of a Jewish mother but a Gentile father – constitute an additional "tribe."

The clearest topic that illustrates such a dispute is a very theoretical question – may the child of a converted man and an Israelite woman marry a *mamzer* (as a convert may)? This matter is debated

between two of the leading halachic codes – the Tur, representing
the Tosafist tradition, and the Shulchan Aruch, who almost quotes
Rambam verbatim.[1]

The Shulchan Aruch[2] states:

גר שנשא בת ישראל, או ישראל שנשא גיורת, הולד ישראל לכל דבר ואסור
בממזרת.

If a convert marries a [born] Jewess or a [born] Jew marries a convert,
the child is an Israelite for all matters and may not marry a *mamzer*.

The Tur,[3] however, states:

כהנים לוים וישראלים מותרים זה בזה, והולד הולך אחר הזכר: בן הכהן כהן בן
הלוי לוי בן הישראל ישראל. . . . גר . . . שנשא לויה או ישראלית . . . הולד הולך
גם כן אחר הזכר, לא שנא גר שנשא ישראלית או ישראל שנשא גיורת.

Priests, Levites and Israelites can marry each other, and the child
follows the [tribal] identification of the father: the child of a priest is a
priest and the child of a Levite is a Levite and the child of an Israelite
is an Israelite. . . . If a convert . . . marries a Levite or Israelite woman
. . . the child follows the status of the man – it makes no difference
whether a convert man marries an Israelite woman or an Israelite man
marries a convert woman.

The Tur, in contrast to the Shulchan Aruch, states that the child of a
converted man is a *ger*. The status of convert can be inherited from
one's father.[4] The position of the Tur traces back through his father,
the Rosh, to the Tosafists. Tosafot understand one's status as a *ger*
to be exactly like one's status as a Levite or Israelite – it is passed on
through the father as an almost tribal status. A *ger* is a Jew whose
male ancestors did not stand at Mt. Sinai with Moses.

That the two views conceptualize converts and born-Jews very
differently is further made clear by the Ran, a later *Rishon* of the

---

1. For Rambam, see Atzai Arazim as quoted in Otzar Haposkim 8:3.
2. ShA EH 4:23 and EH 8:3.
3. Tur EH 8.
4. This same dispute is, I think, what lies behind both sides of a complex
teshuva of the Noda Beyehuda as to whether a child of a woman who converts
while pregnant (with the child in utero) is considered a born-Jew or a convert;
see Dagul M'revava 268 and Pitchai Teshuva 268:6. One view says that this child
cannot be a convert, since they were born to a Jewish mother – and others do not
see that as an obstacle to being considered a *ger*.

Spanish neo-Tosafist school. The Ran states explicitly that the Rambam makes no sense to him:[5]

וכתב הרמב"ם ז"ל בפרק ט"ו מהלכות אסורי ביאה ... "גר שנשא בת ישראל הולד ישראל גמור ואסור בממזרת". ולא ידעתי מנין לו. דאע"ג דעובד כוכבים הבא על בת ישראל הולד ישראל גמור ואסור בממזרת, התם היינו טעמא משום לפי שאי אפשר לו להתייחס אחר אביו – דלמשפחותם לבית אבותם בישראל הוא דכתיב. אבל זה שאביו ישראל גמור למה לא יתיחס אחר אביו, ויהא נדון כגר דמותר בממזרת? והרי כאן יש [דף סו ב] קידושין ואין עבירה והולד הולך אחר הזכר! וצ"ע.

Rambam states in Issurai Biah ch.15 ... "A convert who marries a Jewess, the child is a Jew and prohibited to a *mamzer*." I do not know how he derived this. Although when a Gentile fathers a child with a Jewess the child is Jewish and prohibited to a *mamzer*, there the reason is because the child cannot follow his father's status – since the verse "by their families, the house of their fathers" is limited to Jewish men. However, why should one whose father is Jewish not follow the status of his father, and let this person be considered a *ger* who is permitted to a woman *mamzer*. [After all, the general rule is that] when there is a valid marriage and no sin, the child follows the father['s status]. This remains problematic.

Ran is so convinced of the Tosafist conceptualization that he does not grasp that the Rambam apparently understands that the status of *ger* is a personal status that derives only from the circumstances of one's own life (*horato v'leydato shelo bikedusha*).

Inasmuch as the debate revolves around the irresolvable question of whether the status of *ger* is inheritable, Chelkat Mechukek, Bet Shmuel, Avnei Meluim, and Aruch Hashulchan all remain uncertain as to how to rule in this situation (although it is almost never relevant, as we have almost no identified *mamzerim* who are looking to marry converts).[6]

---

5. Kiddushin (30b Rif pages).
6. See Chelkat Mechukek (4:23), Bet Shmuel (4:37 and 8:2), Avnei Meluim (4:15) and Aruch Hashulchan (8:2).

Marriage between a *Giyoret* and a Kohen

A way to test whether these differing conceptualizations are absolute is to compare them to the following Tannaitic and Amoraic debates and to the *Rishonim*'s positions thereon. In general terms, some Tannaim – such as Rabbi Meir and Rabbi Yehudah – consider converts and their families a separate congregation from the three congregations of priests, of Levites, and of Israelites, but other sages consider converts fully part of the congregation of Jews.[7]

In practical terms: Rabbi Yehuda not only instructs converts to avoid marrying each other[8] instead of marrying with born-Jews; moreover, he rules that the daughter of an actual convert father (or even of a father both of whose parents were converts) is still not fit to marry a Kohen. Rabbi Eliezer b. Yaakov rules more leniently, that as long as at least one of a woman's parents is not a convert – including the daughter of both a convert and of a cultural insider – she is fit to marry a Kohen. Rabbi Yosi, in line with the other sages, rules that even a Jewess born to two actual convert parents is fit to marry a Kohen. In the words of the Mishnah:[9]

רבי יהודה אומר בת גר זכר כבת חלל זכר.

רבי אליעזר בן יעקב אומר ישראל שנשא גיורת בתו כשרה לכהונה וגר שנשא בת ישראל בתו כשרה לכהונה, אבל גר שנשא גיורת בתו פסולה לכהונה ...

אפילו עד עשרה דורות – עד שתהא אמו מישראל.

רבי יוסי אומר אף גר שנשא גיורת בתו כשרה לכהונה.

Rabbi Yehuda says: the daughter of a convert father is equivalent to the daughter of a disqualified son of a priest [i.e., is forbidden to Kohanim].

Rabbi Eliezer b. Yaakov says: [both] the daughter of an Israelite man who married a convert woman and the daughter of a convert man who married a woman of an Israelite family are fit for [marriage into] the priesthood. However, the daughter of a convert man who married a convert woman is unfit for [marriage into] the priesthood . . . forever – until [at least] the mother is of an Israelite family.

Rabbi Yosi says: even the daughter of a convert man who married a convert woman is fit for [marriage into] the priesthood.

---

7. Tosefta Kiddushin 5:1.
8. Tosefta Kiddushin 5:2.
9. Mishnah Kiddushin 4:6–7, Bavli 77a.

There are more permutations on these positions among the *Tannaim* and *Amoraim*. For example: the *Tanna*, Rabbi Shimon b. Yochai, ruled that even a woman who had converted as an infant is fit to marry a Kohen.[10] The *Amora*, Rav, ruled that daughters are affected by mothers and that a woman is unfit to marry a priest as long as she is a daughter of a daughter of a woman convert regardless of how many generations and regardless of born-Jewish fathers along the way.[11] However, if we focus on the *Amoraic* discussion as found in the Bavli, we find the following positions:

אמר רב המנונא משמיה דעולא: הלכה כרבי יוסי.

וכן אמר רבה בר בר חנה: הלכה כרבי יוסי, ומיום שחרב בית המקדש נהגו כהנים סילסול בעצמן כרבי אליעזר בן יעקב.

אמר רב נחמן, אמר לי הונא: בא לימלך, מורים לו כרבי אליעזר בן יעקב. נשא, אין מוציאים אותה ממנו כרבי יוסי.

Rav Hamnunah said in the name of Ulla: the halacha is in accordance with Rabbi Yosi [who permits the daughter of converts and a Kohen to marry].

So, too, Rabbah b. Bar Chanah said: the halacha is in accordance with Rabbi Yosi. Nonetheless, from the time of the Temple's destruction priests pridefully conducted themselves in accordance with Rabbi Eliezer b. Yaakov.

Rav Nachman [however] states: Huna told me, "If one comes to consult we direct him in accordance with Rabbi Eliezer b. Yaakov. If he married, we don't take her away – in accordance with Rabbi Yosi."

In other words, *Tannaim* and *Amoraim* debated whether one who is born to converts – in contrast to one born to a family lacking converts – is an Israelite or at least is, as a woman, fit to marry a Kohen – or at least to stay married.

When we turn to the *Rishonim*, we discover the following: Rambam appears to rule in accordance with his previous view that the daughter of converts is an Israelite woman (who is forbidden to marry a *mamzer*). Although he forbids a Kohen to marry a daughter of converts, he rules that there is no grounds for divorce if the Kohen did so.[12] This is in line with a reading in which Ulla and Rabbah b. Bar Chanah follow Rabbi Yosi and in which Rabbah b. Bar Chanah rejects

---

10. Sifrei Bamidbar #157; Yerushalmi Kiddushin 4:6; Bavli 78a.
11. Rav Hamnunah in the name of Rav (Yerushalmi Kiddushin 4:6).
12. MT Forbidden Relations 19:12.

the prideful priestly behavior, while Rav Nachman in the name of Huna praises it but does not view it as required. The Tosafist through neo-Tosafist tradition, however, may understand both that Rabbah b. Bar Chanah looked upon the priestly practice favorably and that Rav Nachman in the name of Huna actually forbid the marriage even de facto; even as the courts do not compel the couple to divorce, their children are viewed as possibly (literally, doubtfully) disqualified children of Kohanim (who should be avoided by Kohanim).[13] In other words, it views the daughter of converts as a convert. We have no incontrovertible evidence for this understanding of their position, but that is easily their position and would match their position above.

In truth, the question of defined status for marriage may not be most relevant to determining whether the children of a convert have special rights of protection – similar to those of actual converts. After all, it is clear that there is some dispute about the status of children of converts (as in Tosafists permitting the child of two converts to marry a *mamzer* while not forcing a Kohen who is married to the daughter of two converts to divorce her and as in the range of interim *Tannaitic* and *Amoraic* positions regarding marriage between a Kohen and a daughter of converts or of a convert father or of a convert). We have not only seen in the previous essay that the definitions are not identical across all the halachic areas of the one topic of a convert serving as a judge. Rather, as the Pri Megadim states[14] in commenting on the Magen Avraham's point[15] that there is an additional Biblical obligation to love a convert beyond the basic Biblical obligation to love a fellow Jew, the requirement to love a convert has more to do with his or her reality of being a stranger in the community of Jews than with a defined status – and this reality can easily apply to the children of two converts, too:

ומה שכתב אהבת הגר ב' מצות עשה . . . מסתברא דגר מקרי אף הורתו ולידתו
בקדושה, שנתגיירו אביו ואמו, הואיל ואין לו קרובים בישראל.

Regarding that which [t]he [Magen Avraham] wrote, that loving a convert involves two Biblical obligations . . . it seems sensible that even a person conceived and born after the parents converted to Judaism is considered a *ger*, since [s/]he has no relatives among the Jews.

---

13. For more on this, see Pitchai Teshuva 4:3.
14. OC Eshel Avraham 156:2.
15. Magen Avraham 156:2.

Conclusion

Is the son or daughter of two converts (or of one convert – whether of a convert father, according to some, or of a convert mother, according to others) a *ger*? In general, Rambam and Shulchan Aruch are of the view that the status of a *ger* applies only to one who actually converted (even as some restrictions can apply to the children). In general, the Tosafist tradition is of the view that being a *ger* can be a familial status – similar to being a Kohen, Levi, or Israelite; one is a *ger* if one's parents are *gerim*, and maybe even if just one's father is a *ger* (although such distinction is not always enforced *de facto*). Many details of Jewish law hinge on this dispute, and the definitions appear to be context dependent. That being the case, the simplest way to summarize an answer is through the following two points: *lechatchelah* we are generally strict for both views – at least for male converts. When it comes to the special obligation to love the convert, the reality of alienation within the community and the concurrent need for extra care are the critical factors in determining whether the obligation applies.

May the Daughter of a Gentile Man and a Jewish Woman Marry a Kohen?

Preface

At first glance, the reader may wonder what this essay has to do with the themes of this work. Upon finishing this essay, however, one understands that it is worth including for five distinctly different reasons. First, this essay fosters a deeper understanding of the reasons why a Kohen cannot marry a convert. Second, it enhances the reader's understanding of who is and who is not considered a convert as a matter of Jewish law. Third, it gives one a more nuanced understanding of how Jewish law constructs rules that are "best practice" (*lechatchela*) and also when something is "acceptable in time of need" (*bedeeved*), a common notation in this work. Fourth, this essay provides insight into how many *Rishonim* and *Achronim* resolve difficult cases where the *gemara* is unclear, something which is regularly done in this work. Finally, cases like this one are very common when someone thinks that they have had a valid conversion and marry within the Jewish community, and then the validity of the conversion is rightfully questioned, leading to a situation where a man thinks he is Jewish, but actually is not. For all these reasons, this essay is included in this work.

Introduction

Jewish life in the United States is subject to two trends that seem to be pointing in opposite directions. The first is an astonishingly high intermarriage and assimilation rate,[1] which is causing the Orthodox

---

1. According to data from the National Jewish Population Survey of 2000–2001, 47% of Jews who married in the last five years married non-Jews – up from

community to encounter families in our midst in which the husband is not Jewish. The second phenomenon – pointing in the exact opposite direction – is the incredibly large number of *baalei teshuvah*, people who are returning to living a life committed to halacha,[2] including sons and daughters from such families. This essay examines one question that arises from that intersection – whether a Kohen may marry the daughter of a Gentile man and a Jewish woman. Although this question is not a matter of conversion, in addressing the very important issue of the status of a person whose father is a Gentile we also address many matters related to conversion.

This essay is divided into four sections. The first section discusses the Talmudic sources on this topic. The second section surveys the *Rishonim's* discussion of this topic. The third section examines the codification of this halacha in the Shulchan Aruch Code of Law and in its many commentators. The third section also examines how this issue is understood among the post-Shulchan Aruch commentators, codifiers, and responsa writers. The final section surveys contemporary halachic authorities on this issue and reflects both on the differences between inreach and outreach and between the halachic cultures of Israel and of the United States.

I.   THE TALMUDIC SOURCES

As is well known, the Torah explicitly forbids marrying Jewish sons off to Gentile women,[3] and halacha considers the offspring of such union to be Gentiles.[4] As regards the offspring of Jewish women, however, there is a multi-generational Tannaitic and Amoraic debate: Is the offspring of a Gentile father and a Jewish mother Jewish but a *mamzer* – forbidden in marriage to all born-Jews of good standing – or not a *mamzer*? This led to a second question: If the offspring of a Gentile father and a Jewish mother is not forbidden to all born-Jews

---

a readjusted intermarriage figure of 43% from the previous survey (1990). The overall intermarriage rate has grown tremendously over the past 30 years, from an average of 9% before 1965 to 52% in 1990. By 2013, the intermarriage rate was even higher (http://www.pewresearch.org/daily-number/intermarriage-on-the-rise-in-the-u-s/).

2. NJPS data indicates that about 19% of Orthodox Jews in America were not raised Orthodox.

3. Devarim 7:3.

4. Shulchan Aruch 8:5.

of good standing, is such a daughter forbidden to a Kohen, and to what degree?

The Talmudic sources begin with a mishna,[5] that teaches as a blanket statement that the offspring is a *mamzer*, and with a tosefta,[6] that cites a *Tannaitic* debate over the matter:

בת ישראל לכהן ובת כהן לישראל וילדה הימנו בת והלכה הבת ונישאת לעבד או
לגוי וילדה הימנו בן הרי זה ממזר

The son of a [Jewish] woman [of good familial standing[7]] and her slave or Gentile husband is a *mamzer*.

גוי ועבד הבאו על בת ישראל והולידה בן הולד ממזר

ר' שמעון בן יהודה אומ' משם ר' שמעון אין ממזר אלא מן האשה שאיסורה
איסור ערוה וחייבין עליה כרת

The son of a Jewish woman and a Gentile or a slave is a *mamzer*.

R. Shimon b. Yehuda says in the name of R. Shimeon: only one born of a woman forbidden [to the father] as ervah with a liability of excision [i.e., born of close relatives or of adultery] is a *mamzer*.

The Jerusalem Talmud Yevamot 4:15 (6c) and the Babylonian Talmud in Yevamot 44b–45a recount that Amoraim continued to debate the matter, but point out that all sages agreed that such a daughter is forbidden in marriage to a Kohen:

אף על גב דרבי שמעון בן יהודה משום ר' שמעון גוי ועבד שבאו על בת ישראל
הולד כשר, מודי שאם היתה נקיבה שהיא פסולה מן הכהונה . . .

אף על גב דרב אמר גוי ועבד שבאו על בת ישראל הולד כשר, מודי שאם
היתה נקיבה שהיא פסולה מן הכהונה . . .

Although Rabbi Shimon b. Judah rules in the name of R. Shimeon that the offspring of a Gentile or slave and a Jewish woman is legitimate (*kasher*), he admits that a daughter is ineligible (*pesulah*) to a Kohen. . . .

Although Rav rules that the offspring of a Gentile or slave and a Jewish woman is legitimate (*kasher*), he admits that a daughter is ineligible (*pesulah*) to a Kohen. . . .

אמר רבה בר בר חנה א"ר יוחנן: הכל מודים, בעבד ועובד כוכבים הבא על בת
ישראל, שהולד ממזר.

---

5. Mishnah Yevamot 7:5.

6. Tosefta Yevamot 4:16.

7. More precisely: a woman whose mother is the daughter of a Kohen or an Israelite and whose father is a Kohen or an Israelite.

אמר רב יוסף: רבותא למחשב גברי? הא רב ושמואל בבבל, ורבי יהושע בן
לוי ובר קפרא בארץ ישראל, ואמרי לה חלופי בר קפרא ועיילי זקני דרום, דאמרי:
עובד כוכבים ועבד הבא על בת ישראל - הולד כשר!

כי אתא רב דימי אמר: רבי יצחק בר אבודימי משום רבינו אמרו עובד כוכבים
ועבד הבא על בת ישראל - הולד ממזר.

רבי יהושע בן לוי אומר: הולד מקולקל.

למאן? אילימא לקהל, הא אמר רבי יהושע: הולד כשר!
אלא לכהונה.

דכולהו אמוראי דמכשרי מודו שהולד פגום לכהונה - מק"ו מאלמנה: מה
אלמנה לכהן גדול שאין איסורה שוה בכל, בנה פגום; זו שאיסורה שוה בכל, אינו
דין שבנה פגום?

Rabbah b. Bar Hanah said in the name of R. Yohanan: All agree that the offspring of a Gentile man and a Jewish woman is a *mamzer*...

R. Yosef said: ... Rav and Shmuel in Babylonia and R. Yehoshua b. Levi and Bar Kappara in the Land of Israel ... said: the offspring is *kasher*...

When R. Dimi came (from Palestine to Babylonia), he stated:

R. Yitzchak ben Avudimi said in the name of the masters: They have said that if an idolater or a slave had intercourse with the daughter of an Israelite, the child [born] is a *mamzer*.

R. Yehoshua ben Levi said: The child is damaged (*mekulkal*).

[The Gemara asks: damaged] to whom? If we mean to the whole congregation, R. Yehoshua ben Levi had previously stated that the child is legitimate!

Rather, [he meant that the child is damaged] to a Kohen.

After all, even the Amoraim who declare the child legitimate all agree that he is *pagum* (impaired, unfit). This is inferred *a fortiori* (*kal vachomer*) from the case of a widow. If the son of a widow who was married to a Kohen Gadol is impaired – [the son of] a prohibited relationship that is not equally applicable to all [since Jewish men, in general, are not prohibited to marry a widow], how much more should the son of this woman [and an idolater or slave father] be impaired – [inasmuch as] the prohibition is equally applicable to all.

The Jerusalem Talmud argues that all *Amoraim* agree that the daughter of a Gentile father is invalid (*pesulah*) to a Kohen. The Babylonian Talmud uses a slightly different word for impaired (*pegumah*) – but also both compares such offspring to the invalid offspring of a Kohen Gadol and a widow, and states in passing that even such a son is impaired (which would seem to mean that he passes such invalidity on to his daughter – similarly to other classic invalid *chalalim*).

At this point, it is easy to conclude that the daughter of a Gentile man and a Jewish woman is in fact forbidden to a Kohen just as a divorcee or a convert is forbidden to a Kohen, and as a widow is forbidden to a Kohen Gadol. Accordingly, when the Babylonian Talmud ends the whole discussion (page 45b) with the ruling that the offspring of a Jewish mother and a Gentile father are *kasher*, it means acceptable in marriage in general but not to Kohanim. This reading is further reinforced by the fact that the last *Amoraic* ruling that the Gemara cites before its own concluding ruling seems to address those who would think that such offspring should not be *kasher* at all:

א"ל רב אחא בריה דרבה לרבינא: איקלע אמימר לאתרין, ואכשר בין בפנויה בין באשת איש.

והלכתא: עובד כוכבים ועבד הבא על בת ישראל - הולד כשר, בין בפנויה בין באשת איש.

R. Acha son of Rabbah said to Ravina: Amemar once happened to be in our place, and he declared [a] child [of a Gentile father] to be legitimate in the case of a married woman [who had adulterous relations with him] and [not only] in the case of an unmarried woman.

And the halacha is that (*vehilcheta*) if an idolater or a slave cohabited with the daughter of an Israelite, the child [born from such a union] is legitimate (*kasher*), both in the case of a married woman, and in that of an unmarried woman.

Inasmuch as the *Tannaim* and *Amoraim* debated (above) whether the offspring of a Gentile father and Jewish mother is at all *kasher*, and given that Amemar discusses the offspring of even an adulterous Jewish woman and her Gentile paramour, it seems clear that the permissive ruling is only about general marriage fitness – and not about fitness to a Kohen.

There is another way, however, to read this passage. Although the Jerusalem Talmud explicitly says that such daughter is *pesulah* – and the two Talmuds do appear congruent here[8] – the Jerusalem Talmud[9] and various *Rishonim*[10] use the word *pasul* itself with differing shades of meaning in different contexts. Similarly, the Babylonian Talmud uses the word *pagum* at times to mean a slight injunction or even

---

8. As Rabbi Joseph Karo writes (Kessef Mishneh, Gerushin 13:18), "Interpreting the Bavli so as to prevent it from arguing with the Yerushalmi is better, even if the explanation is a bit forced (קצת דחוק)."

9. For example: Yevamot 7:6 (8b).

10. For example: Rashba, Ritva, and Meiri on Yevamot 45a – alluding to Rashi ad loc., s.v. *bitah*. Cf. Avnei Nezer 16.

merely inappropriate.[11] Thus, *pasul* or *pagum* in this context might mean rabbinically forbidden at a low level. The passing reference to the son of a Gentile woman as also impaired might be a mere colloquial reference to offspring – meaning in our case a daughter. The comparison of the daughter of a Jewish woman and a Gentile father to the offspring of a widow and a Kohen Gadol might only be a way of pointing out that Kohanim have higher standards that should make it inappropriate to marry the daughter of a Gentile father and Jewish mother, rather than an argument that the offspring of a Gentile father is seriously invalid and that such a son can pass the invalidity on to his daughter.

Without entering at this point into proofs that one might offer by analyzing whether the Talmud could have really meant to compare the daughter of a Jewish mother from a Gentile father to the daughters and sons of a Kohen who married sinfully, this reading is made likely by the fact that the passage's last Amoraic ruling, from Amemar, permits the child of even an adulterous Jewish woman and her Gentile father; Amemar simply ignores a Gentile father. Thus, the Gemara's concluding ruling (45b) that the offspring of a Gentile father and a Jewish woman is *kasher* means absolutely *kasher*; the Gemara does not even bother to discuss again whether such a daughter is permitted to a Kohen – she obviously is permitted:

א"ל רב אחא בריה דרבה דרבה לרבינא: איקלע אמימר לאתרין, ואכשר בן בפנויה בין באשת איש.

והלכתא: עובד כוכבים ועבד הבא על בת ישראל, הולד כשר – בין בפנויה בין באשת איש.

And the halacha is (*vehilcheta*): if an idolater or a slave cohabited with the daughter of an Israelite, the child [born from such a union] is legitimate (*kasher*) – both in the case of a married woman and in that of an unmarried woman.

The Gemara concludes by saying that the offspring of a Gentile man and a Jewish woman is *kasher*. There are no limiting qualifications.

II. THE *RISHONIM*'S FIVE POSSIBLE EXPLANATIONS OF THE TALMUD

Rishonim take, in broad outline, five different views of understanding the practical halacha derived from this Talmudic discussion.

---

11. In this case, even a forced reading is unnecessary.

- One view is that although the daughter of a Gentile man and a Jewish woman is a Jewess, she is seriously forbidden to a Kohen. After all, the Talmud never revoked its qualification that such offspring is forbidden to a Kohen even if *kasher* to other Jews.

- A second view from the same medieval rabbinic tradition – a view that is generally ignored – is that even when the Talmud states that the offspring is *kasher* it only means that such son or daughter is a Gentile who can marry his or her mother's fellow Jews upon his or her conversion. Thus, a daughter is invalid to a Kohen inasmuch as a *giyoret* is invalid to a Kohen.

- A third view rules that the permissibility of marriage between a Kohen and the daughter of a Gentile father is under doubt in Jewish law. Perhaps the Talmud did not comment at the end on the question of marriage to a Kohen because the injunction is clear, and perhaps it did not comment at the end because a special injunction was obviously no longer conceivable and she is permitted to a Kohen.

- A fourth view – from the strict tradition – interprets this doubt as a serious doubt of law. It thus demands that a Kohen divorce a wife born of a Gentile father, even as it does not allow the courts to compel the Kohen husband to divorce.

- A fifth view is that the offspring of a Gentile man and a Jewish woman is *kasher* to all Jews – including to a Kohen. The Talmud rules thus without qualification.

- A minor view, following the lenient tradition, both supports the fourth view in theory and in practice radically weakens the injunction even according to the practice of forbidding such marriage due to doubt. It argues that the Talmud text does seem to overturn the injunction, which in any case is a minor rabbinic prohibition that prohibits the woman alone as inappropriate to a Kohen – but cannot apply to grandchildren and is not a strict prohibition.

The five major views, as elaborated, are as follows.

A. THE ROSH'S POSITION: THE DAUGHTER OF A GENTILE MAN IS STRICTLY FORBIDDEN TO A KOHEN

The last leading *Rishon* of the French-German High Medieval rabbinic tradition, the Rosh (Yevamot 4:30), maintains that the daughter of a Gentile man and a Jewish mother is strictly forbidden to a Kohen. He writes:

מדקאמר לעיל סתמא דגמרא דכולהו אמוראי דמכשרו מודו דהולד פגום לכהונה
ק"ו מאלמנה וכו' וכיון דק"ו לית ליה פירכא ליכא מאן דפליג עליה ומה שלא
הזכיר הגמרא בכאן והלכתא הולד פגום משום דלא צריך למיפסק דכבר מסיק
סתמא דגמרא לעיל דכולהו אמוראי מודו דבנה פגום דליכא מאן דפליג ולא
הוצרך לפסוק אלא שהולד כשר לקהל ואפי' באשת איש:

The Talmud plainly stated earlier, "All *Amoraim* who declare the
child legitimate agree that he is *pagum*. This is inferred *a fortiori* (*kal
vachomer*) from the case of a widow." Since that *kal vachomer* is not
refuted, nobody disputes it. [Thus,] the reason that the Talmud did
not explicitly state in its concluding ruling that the child is *pagum* is
because it was not necessary; it had stated above that all *Amoraim* who
declare the child legitimate agree that he is *pagum*, with no dispute.
The only matter that the Talmud still needed to rule upon was that
such a child [of a Gentile father] is in fact permitted to marry into the
congregation of Israel – even if his mother had been married to a Jew
[concurrently].

The Rosh understands the conclusion of the Gemara that the child is
kasher to mean that the child is a Jewish non-*mamzer* who can marry
fellow Jews in general but is ineligible to marry a Kohen. The statement that "all *Amoraim* who declare the child legitimate agree that
he is *pagum*" was never superseded inasmuch as both the unanimous
rulings forbidding such marriage and the *kal vachomer* advanced by
the Gemara to support the prohibition were never debated in the
Gemara.

B. A TOSAFIST VIEW: THE DAUGHTER OF A GENTILE MAN AND A JEWISH WOMAN IS A GENTILE (AND THUS IS FORBIDDEN TO A KOHEN)

A novel approach to this injunction raised in France earlier in
Tosafot on Kiddushin 75b[12] was restated in Kitzur Piskei Tosafot
on Kiddushin.[13] This view posits that when the Talmud states that
the offspring of a relationship between a Gentile man and a Jewish
woman is valid (*kasher*), it merely means that he or she is not per-
manently forbidden to born-Jews of good standing as a *mamzer/et*.
Rather, he or she is a valid Gentile who can marry into the mother's
people after accepting Judaism – after converting:

---

12. s.v. ve-Rabbi Yishmael.
13. *Asarah Yuchasin*, no. 142.

... אם הולד כשר א"כ הוא הולך אחר העובד כוכבים כדאמר בס"פ דלעיל ...
וליכא למיחש לכך אם תנשא לעובד כוכבים ...

... If the offspring is *kasher* that means that it goes after the Gentile
[father] ... and it matters not if she [i.e. such daughter] gets married
to a gentile ...

אם עובד כוכבים הבא על בת ישראל הולד כשר, הוי עובד כוכבים

If the offspring of a Gentile man and a Jewish woman is *kasher*, they
are Gentiles.

According to this view, *kasher* cannot mean valid to marry a Kohen.
The son or daughter of a Gentile father is a Gentile fit to marry
Gentiles unless he or she converts, and a convert cannot marry a
Kohen. However, Pitchei Teshuvah has already noted that this view
is rejected by nearly all halachic authorities.[14] It is generally not even
factored into the halachic calculus at all.

C. THE RIF'S POSITION: IT IS UNCERTAIN IF THE DAUGHTER OF A GENTILE MAY MARRY A KOHEN

In truth, this question of law had been debated earlier between the
Geonim.[15] Accordingly, the teacher of the Rambam's father's teacher
– the Rif – pointed out that some of his teachers permit a marriage
between a Kohen and the daughter of a Gentile father while others
forbid it. He then concludes:[16]

ואנן מספקא לן אי אי הוי פגום אי לא מדחזינן לגמרא בתר שקלא וטריא דפסק
והלכתא עובד כוכבים ועבד הבא על בת ישראל הולד כשר ולא אמר והלכתא
הולד פגום:

But we are uncertain as to whether this woman is *pagum* or not, from
the fact that we see the Gemara, after much give-and-take, rules that
"the halacha is that if an idolater or a slave had cohabited with the
daughter of an Israelite the child [born from such a union] is legitimate (*kasher*)," but it did not say that the child is *pagum*.

---

14. Pitchei Teshuvah, Even HaEzer 4:1. For example: Rif, Rambam, Rosh,
Ramban, Meiri, Ritva, Beit Shmuel, Chelkat Mechokek, Shach, Taz, Aruch
Hashulchan, and Noda Bi-Yehudah all reject this view.
15. See Otzar Ha-Geonim p. 106, in the name of Baal Meitav and Bahag.
16. Yevamot 15a in Rif pagination.

The Rif writes that because of the lack of clarity in the Gemara's conclusion the matter remains a legal doubt (*safek*). The tension between the Talmud's seemingly blanket conclusion that the child of a Gentile man and Jewish woman is *kasher*, on the one hand, and the Talmud's earlier assessment that the Amoraim who rule that such a child is allowed to marry a Jew concede that she is not to marry a Kohen, on the other hand, produces a condition of doubt.

D. THE RAMBAN'S POSITION

The Ramban, as the rabbinic figure who combined the French-German Tosafist tradition with the Spanish rabbinic tradition, understood the Rif to have recognized that those *Amoraim* who did forbid a Kohen to marry the daughter of a Gentile father, forbade it as a serious sin. Thus, the upshot of the Rif's ruling that this matter of Biblical law stands in legal doubt is to rule strictly on all related questions. As the Ramban writes in his Sefer ha-Zechut on the Rif, this means the following: a Kohen may not marry the daughter of a Gentile man and a Jewish woman since she may be forbidden (*safek chalalah*). If the Kohen did so, he is religiously obligated to divorce her since she may be forbidden. If he had children with her, the sons' daughters are also forbidden to a Kohen due to doubt about the sons' status (*safek chalal*[17]) – and yet the sons, themselves, may not come in contact with a corpse since they might be Kohanim.

In spite of this strict reading of the Rif with its strict religious demands, however, the Ramban does not overturn Spanish tradition. He notes that if a Kohen and the daughter of a Gentile father do marry – in contravention of the halacha – the couple cannot be compelled to divorce since the law is in doubt.[18] As a number of *Achronim* explain: the couple ought to get divorced, but the courts cannot force them to do so since courts may only force a man to divorce when the law obligates him to divorce, and forcing a husband to do so under other conditions (*get me'useh*) simply results in an invalid divorce; in such a case, the divorce would be doubtfully invalid or valid and thus invalid in practice.[19]

---

17. Of course this is not a classic case of *chalal* inasmuch as the child does not result from a sexually improper union with a Kohen.

18. Why this is so will be explained below.

19. See Pitchei Teshuvah, Even HaEzer 4:3.

E. THE RAMBAM'S POSITION: THE DAUGHTER OF A GENTILE MAN MAY MARRY A KOHEN

This was the Rambam's understanding of the Rif. It incorporates the French-German rabbinic understanding that the Talmud seriously forbids a Kohen to marry the daughter of a Gentile father even as it maintains the Spanish tradition of accepting the authority of the Rif.

The Rif's actual position, however, may have been different. And, if so, it may be revealed best by the Rambam. After all, the Rambam was a son of a student of the Rif's student. As such, he could be expected to reflect the Rif's tradition. Furthermore, the Rambam's own codification becomes much clearer if we accept that he followed the Rif.

In his code (Hil. Issurei Biah 15:3), the Rambam codifies only the concluding line of the Gemara without qualification: The Rambam writes:

עכו"ם ועבד הבא על בת ישראל הולד כשר – בין פנויה בין באשת איש בין באונס בין ברצון.

> The child of a Gentile man or a male slave who had relations with a Jewish woman is *kasher*, whether the woman was unmarried or [even] married, whether it was forced or [even] consensual.

The Rambam maintains without qualification that one whose father is a Gentile is eligible. This has generally been understood halachically to mean that the Rambam permits a Kohen to marry the daughter of a Gentile father.[20] Accordingly, the Rambam must understand that the Babylonian Talmud's closing ruling supersedes the earlier Amoraic limitations that placed some stigma (*pegimah*) on the offspring of a Gentile father and Jewish mother.

---

20. This understanding of the Rambam is nearly universally accepted, although the Rosh' student, Mishneh Le-Melech, reads Rambam as agreeing with the Rosh (discussed below). A close examination of both the language of the Rambam and the deep consensus among commentaries on the Rambam, from the Beit Yosef through the Magid Mishneh to the Migdal Oz and even the German Haghahot Maimoniot – among many others – reveals that the Mishneh Le-Melech's interpretation of the Rambam to correlate with the Rosh's position is not correct. The simple understanding of the Rambam is the correct one, namely that the child is eligible to marry a Kohen in the Rambam's view. Indeed, the authoritative Beit Yosef quotes that view almost without any thought to the possibility that any other view could be correct, and Chinuch 560 also adopts this view of the Rambam.

The seeming problem with that reading of the Rambam, however, is that this law is written in the context of the laws of *mamzerut*, where Rambam had no reason to comment on the question of marriage to a Kohen. Thus, one could argue that this line might not inform us of the Rambam's position regarding marriage to a Kohen. Moreover, inasmuch as the Rambam both generally builds his code from direct quotes of earlier rabbinic sources (so that there is no reason to expect any elaboration on the quotes) and had a tradition from the Rif that the matter is a question of law (so that he has no source that he could cite on the matter), one could argue that the reason that he never explicitly forbids a Kohen to marry such a daughter anywhere in his code is because the law is unclear.

On the other hand, one cannot simply answer that the Rambam's code is a mere placeholder. One cannot simply answer that since a permissive view does trace back to some of the Geonim (above) and forward to other *Rishonim*,[21] the Rambam's code with its omission of any restriction was utilized as good a representative of the permissive view as any. Not only does such answer belie how Rambam was understood by tradition. Rather, such answer does not address why the Rambam did not care that some less educated judges were apt to err in not realizing that the permissibility of the marriage of a Kohen to a Jewish daughter of a Gentile father is a matter of doubt.

The best answer, therefore, appears to be a substantive answer. Rambam may have felt no need to state the Rif's doubt – felt no need to break from his standard method of codification – because the doubt is not a serious doubt. While learned Kohanim, those who study Talmud or the Rif carefully would know to avoid such marriages, it did not matter if others did not do so. In other words: Rambam through omission did allow the practice to most Jews. If his tradition taught him that it is a matter of doubt, it apparently also taught him that the Amoraic prohibition against such marriage was not a serious prohibition and that the doubt need not be publicized. According to this perspective: even if the Rambam did not explicitly rule that such marriage is permitted, he also did not care if such marriage was performed since it is not seriously problematic.

This reading of the Rambam, and thus of the Rif, not only explains both the Rambam's coding through omission and why the Ramban had to argue to be strict in avoiding such marriage (etc.) although

---

21. As noted, for example, in the commentaries of the Rashba, Ritva, Meiri on Yevamot 45a.

the Rif had already said that it is a matter of doubt. It not only explains why some viewed the Rif as ruling permissively although he had ruled that it is a matter of doubt;[22] if it is not a serious doubt, it is basically permitted. Rather, it is necessary in order to explain how the Talmud editors (or even Amemar) adopted the right to reject the earlier long-standing consensus that forbade a Kohen to marry the daughter of a Gentile – or even how they possibly rejected that earlier consensus. The editors (or Amemar) could have done so only if the prohibition was not serious.

In any case, this reading is how Maharshal, below, understands the Rif's position.

F.   THE MAHARSHAL'S POSITION: THE DAUGHTER OF A GENTILE MAN IS MERELY DISCOURAGED FROM MARRYING A KOHEN

Although it is impossible to incontrovertibly prove that this last explanation of the Rambam and the Rif was indeed the Rambam's view, it is the Maharshal's understanding of the Talmud and of the Rif. After arguing theoretically that the Gemara does reject the ruling forbidding a Kohen to marry the daughter of a Gentile father, the Maharshal points out that even the Gemara's comparison of the daughter of a Gentile father to other such people who are forbidden to Kohanim for the generations of their descendants (*chalalim*) is not valid when read rigorously.[23] Thus, the Gemara's argument is not a comparison. Rather, it is an allusion to a Kohen's higher marriage standards – which implicitly also forbid a Kohen to marry the daughter of a Gentile father. Nevertheless, the sons of such a forbidden marriage are valid Kohanim.

As he writes in his Yam Shel Shlomo commentary to Yevamot (4:38):[24]

... אין חלל אלא מאיסורי כהונה ...

ולולי דמסתפינא מחברייי הייתי מפרש דעיקר ק"ו דקאמר אינה אלא אסמכתא
בעלמא ואיסורא הוא דעביד אבל אי נשאת אותה הבת לכהן אין הבן מהן חלל
ולא משוינן להאי בת כחללה אלא כפגומה בעלמא ולאסרה היא גופא על הכהן.

---

22. See the Nemukei Yosef's reading of the Rif (ad locum).

23. It is worth noting that there are at least seven distinct problems with the *kal vachomer* put forth by the Gemara in Yevamot 44b. See Ritva, Yevamot col. 251, n. 18 (in vol. 2 of the Mosad Harav Kook edition).

24. That he did not retract this argument later is clear from his referencing it later in Responsa Maharshal #18 (or #17 in some editions).

א"כ כדמסיק תלמודא לקמן והלכתא וכו' הולד כשר, חוזר התלמוד מהאי
סברא ואמר דלית בה איסור כלל ... [ד]השתא דכשר בין בפנויה ובין בא"א
ואפילו מצד ממזר ... ק"ו באיסור פגימה שאינה אלא לכהונה שאתה מכשירו ...
ומ"מ חלילה לי להתיר לכתחילה שיצא בספק מפי הרי"ף. אבל אם נשא, אין
מוציאין מידו וכו"ש שהולד כשר - ולא כדברי הרמב"ן שכתב אין מוציאין והולד ספק.

... A *chalal* [the status of forbidden to a Kohen that is passed on
through sons and that is even recreated through a daughter if a Kohen
has children through such a forbidden wife] only comes about through
people that are [Biblically] forbidden to a Kohen...

And were I not afraid of my colleagues, I would explain that the *a
fortiori* (*kal vachomer*) argument [in the Gemara] is merely an allusion.
A Kohen sins [in marrying a woman born to a Gentile father] but the
son of such marriage is not invalid (not a *chalal*); we do not view this
daughter [of a Gentile] as a *chalala* [i.e., as the daughter of a union between a Kohen and a woman forbidden to him], but rather as unfit – so
that she herself alone is forbidden to a Kohen. Accordingly, when the
Talmud concludes that the offspring [of a Gentile father and a Jewish
woman] is *kasher*, the Talmud retracts this argument and states that
she is not forbidden at all ... for if the offspring of a single and even
[adulterous] married Jewish woman [and a Gentile lover] is *kasher* [not
only to be a Jew but] even as regards [not being a] *mamzer* ... *a fortiori*
that such offspring is *kasher* as regards a prohibition of mere unfitness
for a Kohen alone.

However, God forbid that I should permit that which the Rif declared to be a doubt. Nonetheless, if a Kohen did marry such a woman,
we do not [try to] remove [her] from him and their child is completely
kasher [even as a Kohen] – in contrast to the Ramban who wrote that
we do not remove [her] but the child is of doubtful status.

The Yam Shel Shlomo offers a completely different approach to the
Rif's doubt (and possibly to the Rambam's silence). According to the
Yam Shel Shlomo, the *pegam* only means that such marriage is rabbinically forbidden as despicable or distasteful but not as an absolute
injunction – such as would be passed on to the next generations.
Thus, if a Kohen were to marry such a daughter, not only does the
community have no ability to compel divorce (as the Ramban already stated) but the Kohen and his wife have no religious obligation
to divorce. Rabbinic rulings of this kind are only devised *ab initio*
(*lechatchila*).[25]

---

25. Additional *Acharonim* also maintain that the *pegam* is only *miderabbanan*.

Nor was the Maharshal alone. In Italy, R. Menachem Azaryah (רמ"ע) da Fano (Responsa, No. 124) adopted the view that the *pegam* is only a *pegam miderabbanan* and the term *pegam* denotes only a *lechatchila* prohibition of a rabbinic nature – somewhat analogous to the *pegam* of a woman conceived by a mother who did not purify herself after menstruation; it is merely distasteful and inappropriate. Alongside the Maharshal – whom we shall see below was referenced by leading Polish authorities – the Rema Mipano has also been quoted by many as a reliable ruling.

G. SUMMARY

In summary: in reviewing six *Rishonim's* positions on the question of a Kohen marrying the daughter of a Gentile father, we have seen two major halachic approaches to the question. One view understands that such marriage is seriously forbidden to the point of affecting any children born thereof. Even when a community rules that the prohibition is not to be enforced due to doubt, the Kohen must know that he is obligated to divorce such a woman if he married her and Kohanim must know to avoid marrying that couple's children or forbidden descendants. The other view understands that this is permitted or is merely a matter of a pious prohibition.

II. THE VIEW OF THE CODES, THE COMMENTATORS, AND THE *ACHRONIM*

With our previous discussion as background and our understanding that there are two major halachic approaches to this question, we can now make sense of the codes and the commentators. We will see that some adopt the first view. We will see that others adopt the second view. Moreover, we will see two approaches to a halachic code. Some will read a code as the handiwork of its author, as a work that must be studied in order to understand the author's intent. Others will read a code as a work that has been accepted into their rabbinic culture and thus must be interpreted in line with their rabbinic culture.

The Tur Code (EH 4 and 7), by the son of the Rosh, and R. Yosef Karo's Shulchan Aruch code (EH 4:19 and 7:17), also heavily influ-

---

See Responsa of Rabbi Akiva Eiger, No. 91; Commentary of Beit Meir, Even HaEzer 6:17; Responsa Amudei Or 3:8; Responsa Beit Yitzchak, Even HaEzer 26; and Seridei Esh 3:8.

enced by the Rosh,[26] both state the Rosh's (i.e. the French-German rabbinic tradition's) strict ruling:

עכו"ם ועבד שבא[ו] על ... בת ישראל הולד כשר בין בפנויה בין באשת איש, ופגום לכהונה

If a Gentile or a slave has relations with a . . . single or [even] married Jewish woman, the child is *kasher* – but *pagum* to a Kohen.

As R. Yosef Karo states explicitly in his Beit Yosef commentary on the Tur, this ruling follows the Rosh and uses pagum to mean seriously pasul.

Similarly, the Shulchan Aruch (EH 7:17) rules on this matter again in slightly different wording than the Tur (EH 7) but to the same effect. The Tur and the Shulchan Aruch state, respectively:

עכו"ם ועבד הבא על בת ישראל, אף על פי שהולד כשר לבא בקהל פגום הוא לכהונה

The offspring of a sexual encounter between a Gentile or slave and a Jewish woman is indeed *kasher* to marry into the congregation, but is *pagum* for Kohanim.

עובד כוכבים ועבד הבא על בת ישראל וילדה ממנו בת, אותה הבת פגומה לכהונה.

The daughter born of a sexual encounter between a Gentile or slave and a Jewish woman is *pegumah* for Kohanim.

R. Karo adds in his Beit Yosef commentary that any daughter born to a Kohen and the forbidden daughter of a Gentile daughter is also *pegumah* to a Kohen – i.e., such marriage is a serious sin.

The Rema, however, ruled differently. In his responsa he adopts the same view as his close relative, the Maharshal. He accepts that the offspring of a Gentile man and a Jewish woman is not really pasul to marry a Kohen, but only inappropriate (*pagum umekulkal*).[27] Nonetheless, the Rema writes no disagreeing glosses on these rulings

26. Ta-Shma, Israel M. 1992. "R. Joseph Caro and his *Beit Yosef*: Between Spain and Germany," in Haim Beinart, ed. *Moreshet Sepharad: The Sephardi Legacy – Volume Two*. Jerusalem: Magnes Press, Hebrew University. 194–196 = idem. 1992. "Rabi Yosef Karo ve-Sifro 'Bet Yosef" – Bein Ashkenaz li-Sefarad," in Haim Beinart, ed. *Moreshet Sepharad*. Jerusalem: Magnes Press, Hebrew University. 526–527 (Hebrew).

27. See Shu"t Harema 18; see also 61 and 69.

of the Shulchan Aruch.[28] This silence on the Rema's part reveals a different way of reading the Shulchan Aruch code. It is read as a code for the rabbinic culture that is using it as long as it can be read that way rigorously, regardless of the author's intent. As long as the laws read correctly from the perspective of Polish rabbinic culture, the Rema makes no comments.

This approach is exemplified by the later Eastern European commentaries on the Shulchan Aruch who explicitly read the code to match the lenient approach. For example: Chelkat Mechokek (EH 7:26) states that "the word *pagum* implies that only as an ideal (*lechatchila*) she should not marry a Kohen, but she is not really a *chalalah* – see Maharshal 17." His inference from the word *pagum* is probably based on obvious sources such as the Rambam's (Issurei Bi'ah 15:1) and Shulchan Aruch's (EH 4:13) use of the word *pagum* to refer to the offspring of a woman who did not purify herself before conceiving after menstruation – a use that is understood as not actually forbidding even a Kohen to marry such offspring.[29] (Along the same lines, Chelkat Yaakov EH 32 rules that although the son born of the relationship between a Kohen and a woman whose father was a Gentile could be viewed as a *chashash chalal*, the son – as a matter of basic law [*me'ikar hadin*] is considered a Kohen.)

This method of reading the Shulchan Aruch code in line with one's rabbinic tradition was not necessary, however, for Polish rabbinic authorities to reject the Shulchan Aruch/Rosh position. First, they could simply explain the Shulchan Aruch's positions without adopting a position themselves – as does the Be'er Hagolah EH 4:10. Second, they could simply disagree – or agree – with the Shulchan Aruch. For example: on the one hand, the Bet Shmuel (EH 4:2 and 7:39) both maintains the lenient Polish tradition and recognizes that the Shulchan Aruch follows the strict view that obligates a Kohen to divorce such a woman if he married her sinfully. The Bet Shmuel simply rules that one should not follow the Shulchan Aruch/Rosh – as he also directs the reader to the Maharshal. He even critiques the Rosh (EH 4:4). On the other hand, the Be'er Heitev EH 4:5

---

28. See also Darkei Moshe on Tur, Even HaEzer 7, as well as the notes to *id.* published in the Machon Yerushalayim edition of the Tur which state clearly that Rema adopts the view of the Yam Shel Shlomo.

29. See proofs in Darkei Moshe EH 4:2. The only rabbinic authority who explicitly reads the Rambam as forbidding a Kohen to marry a woman conceived under such conditions is the Levush.

(Polish, but of recent German background and of German tradition) dismisses the Bet Shmuel's argument.[30]

In line with this open evaluation of the debates, leading rabbis from R. Akiva Eiger[31] through Aruch Hashulchan (Even HaEzer 7:35) have discussed the debate between the *Rishonim* and concluded by adopting the lenient view; a Kohen should avoid marrying the daughter of a Gentile father because it is inappropriate, but such marriage is not sinful. This was also the view of the twentieth century Seridei Esh 1:71.[32]

On the other hand, the strict German tradition has also survived. In the twentieth century, the Hungarian Hassidic Minchat Yitzchak 2:131 ruled that the son of a Kohen and the daughter of a Gentile father cannot serve as a Kohen; such a son is a *safek chalal*. Obviously, a daughter is also sinfully invalid to a Kohen – as a matter of doubt (Ramban's view).

Moreover, the strict view even exists – at least in some form – in the Polish-Lithuanian tradition. This is true not only of the independently minded Gra, who after an unusually long discourse on the *Rishonim's* positions concludes that the view of the Rosh or Ramban is correct, that the offspring of a Gentile father is ineligible to a Kohen at least as a matter of uncertainty. Rather, it is also true of other leading rabbis, who distinguished between a not strictly forbidden daughter born of a Gentile man through non-marital sex and the ineligible offspring of a Jewish woman married to a Gentile man (Beit Meir, Even HaEzer 4:4 and see R. Moshe Feinstein below).

IV. THE CONTEMPORARY HALACHIC ISSUE: A KOHEN ROMANTICALLY INVOLVED WITH THE DAUGHTER OF A GENTILE MAN AND A JEWISH WOMAN

The consensus as to the *lechatchela* halacha is clear. The daughter of a Gentile man and a Jewish woman should not marry a Kohen and one should not become romantically involved with someone that one cannot marry *lechatchela*. However, in a situation where such a couple is already romantically involved, what should one do?

Among contemporary halachic authorities this matter has gener-

---

30. For more authorities who debate this issue, see sources in Pitchei Teshuvah EH 4:3.

31. Responsa Mahadura Kama, No. 91.

32. As numbered in the new editions.

ated a three-way dispute. All of them focus on the following question:
A man and woman are already bonded together but not yet married
according to Jewish law; they have now become religious and now
they wish to be married according to Jewish law, but it turns out
that the man is a Kohen and the woman is the child of a relationship
between a Gentile man and Jewish woman. Is it proper for a rabbi to
perform the wedding?

The first authority to answer that question is the late Rav Moshe
Feinstein ztz"l. Rav Moshe says that no rabbi should marry such a
couple. Since the couple is not yet married halachically, this cannot be
considered a situation of *im niseit lo tetze* (if they are already married
they should not get divorced). After all, according to many halachic
authorities a Kohen is better off not being halachically married to a
woman for whom it is prohibited for him to be married to, rather
than marry such a woman *be-chuppah ve-kiddushin*.[33]

---

33. Igrot Moshe EH 1:15. For a detailed explanation of Rav Moshe's view, see
Igrot Moshe, Even HaEzer 1:19, s.v. *umah shebiksheh*. I think Rabbi Feinstein's
strict view here can be well explained in light of another relatively unique view of
his. As explained above, the view of one Tosafot (Kiddushin 75b) is that a child
whose father is a Gentile is a Gentile, even if his mother is Jewish. Nearly all
authorities categorically reject that view (as noted above). Such is not the view of
Rabbi Feinstein. As he notes in Dibrot Moshe on Yevamot 45a, he is of the view
that Tosafot maintains that only when the mother is herself an apostate is the
child a Gentile if the father is. Indeed, in Igrot Moshe, Even HaEzer 1:8, Rabbi
Feinstein accepts this view as a matter of reasonable doubt and rules that such a
child requires a conversion. He states:

> According to what I explained in my novellae in Yevamot, it is the view of
> Tosafot (Kiddushin 75[a]) that if the mother was a Jewess who apostatized,
> then the child has the status of a Gentile like his father. This stands in
> contrast to others who think that according to Tosafot, in every case of a
> sexual relationship between a Gentile man and a Jewish woman the child is
> a Gentile as well, and for that reason, the latter-day authorities are of the
> view that one need not take this opinion of Tosafot into account (see Pitchei
> Teshuvah, Even HaEzer 4:1). Yet according to my explanation that the ruling
> of Tosafot is limited to an apostate Jewess, one certainly should account for
> their view, though now is not the time to elaborate. Therefore, in such a case,
> a full conversion before a *bet din* in accordance with all the laws of conversion
> is required.

Once one is inclined to rule like Tosafot that there are cases where a child
born to a Gentile man and a Jewish woman is actually a Gentile, then it is even
moreso logical to insist that in all cases this child is (as a matter of Torah law)
certainly ineligible to marry a Kohen. On the other hand, those who reject Rabbi
Feinstein's view on this matter with regard to the child of an apostate Jewess and
a Gentile (and nearly all authorities reject his view) ought to be more inclined to

A contrary answer is put forward in works by two Sephardic authorities in the State of Israel where there both is no secular marriage and where the rabbinate must address the needs of secular Jews. Rabbi Shalom Messas in Shemesh UMagen (Even HaEzer 3:58) and the recent Chief Rabbi of Israel, Shlomo Amar, in Shema Shelomoh (Even HaEzer 5:8) both advance the following argument: In any situation in which the couple is already connected to each other – either because they are living together or they are engaged or have set out to plan a wedding, and certainly in a case where if one refuses to perform their marriage ceremony they will get married civilly anyway – that is considered a *bedeeved* situation (or maybe a *shaat hadechak kemo bedeavad* situation) and it is proper to perform such a wedding based on a multi-sided situation of doubt: perhaps the halacha is in accord with the Rambam that such a marriage is permitted; if the halacha is not in accord with the Rambam, perhaps *pagum* means just "distasteful" and not "prohibited"; once the couple is connected, the halacha may very well be that "they need not get divorced." Thus, it is appropriate for a *mesader kiddushin* to perform such a wedding.[34]

R. Ovadia Yosef, also of Israel, ruled similarly in the ninth and tenth volumes of Yabia Omer (Yabia Omer Even HaEzer 9:7, 10:14), but based on a different argument. His view is that there are two distinctly different doubts here. The first doubt is whether the daughter of a Gentile man and a Jewish woman may marry a Kohen, and the second doubt is whether a person is actually considered a Kohen merely because he claims to be a Kohen. According to Rav Ovadia, not only is not clear that some particular Kohanim are actually Kohanim, but the status of almost all Kohanim is a matter of halachic doubt. Together with the vast, systemic doubts about whether this person is really ineligible to marry a Kohen, that gives rise to a case of double doubt and halacha permits this woman to marry a Kohen.[35]

---

consider this child as never having been a Gentile and at most only rabbinically ineligible to a Kohen. It might also be the case that Rabbi Feinstein, on a practical level, solved many of these types of cases by insisting that (as a general proposition) a man from a secular family who claims he is a Kohen actually is not; see Igrot Moshe EH 4:11(1). 4:12, 4:39.

34. See also Yachel Yisrael 96 & 97, who adopts a similar view.

35. As a general matter, there is a dispute among *poskim* as to the status of all modern-day Kohanim. Maharsham (EH 235) and others rule that all Kohanim nowadays are not clearly Kohanim, as there is a general doubt on a Torah level as to everyone's status when claiming to be a Kohen. So too, others note that in a situation where a person claims to be a Kohen but lacks valid proof of such

In truth, even Rav Moshe would easily allow a Kohen from a non-observant family to marry such daughter; he ruled, as a general proposition, that a man from a secular family who claims he is a Kohen actually may not be [Igrot Moshe EH 4:11(1). 4:12, 4:39].

Conclusion

This article addressed the question of whether the daughter of a sexual relationship between a Gentile man and a Jewish woman may marry a Kohen. There is a Talmudic ambiguity on this point, which produced five mainstream views in the *Rishonim* – which we saw could be summarized into two: there is no serious sin or there is a serious sin (at least as a matter of doubt).[36] The Shulchan Aruch and its commentators divide on this issue as well, and the halacha remains somewhat unclear.

As a matter of normative halacha, all modern *poskim* agree that a woman whose father is a Gentile ought not to marry a Kohen since the Shulchan Aruch, Rema and the normative commentators all agree that such conduct is at least distasteful and according to many prohibited. So too, certainly all *poskim* agree that such a woman should be told not to date Kohanim and nearly all *poskim* also agree that if married, such a couple may stay married.

Contemporary halachic authorities do not agree, however, on whether it is proper to perform a halachic marriage ceremony for an already bonded Kohen from a religious background and a woman whose father is a Gentile.[37] Some *poskim* rule that since they are not married yet, they should not marry. Others rule that since there are

---

according to Jewish law (such as testimony from acceptable witnesses), the claim of being a Kohen is discounted. Finally, one finds many contemporary *poskim* who aver that in an immodest generation such as ours, women who are not known to be sexually modest prior to marriage may be assumed to be ineligible to marry a Kohen due to sexual misconduct with a Gentile, and subsequently their children are not Kohanim.

36. Rambam maintains such a child may marry a Kohen, Rosh maintains she may not, Ramban maintains that the matter is in doubt, and Yam Shel Shlomo maintains that the marriage of such a child to a Kohen is distasteful but not prohibited.

37. Either because they are engaged, living together or even civilly married.

many doubts as to whether there is any sin involved, performing such a wedding is permitted.

As to how a rabbi should conduct himself, it seems that it is proper for a rabbi to perform this wedding and bring this couple closer to Judaism in a situation where ruling strictly might drive this couple out of the Orthodox community and away from religious observance generally. As Rav Ovadia Yosef stated in his second responsum dealing with this matter (Yabia Omer Even HaEzer 10:14 – explicitly responding to Rav Moshe's concern that a halachic marriage leads to more sins):

> In my opinion it appears that to the extent that we strive to accept people and arrange a marriage for them on the basis of those *poskim* who rule liberally, they too will see themselves as close to Judaism like every other Jew, and they will become meticulous in their observance of *taharat hamishpacha* (laws of family purity) and immersion in a mikvah and other matters of Judaism. But without this they will consider themselves distant from Judaism and will say in their hearts, "What good would it accomplish for us to keep the mitzvot of the Torah since we are already living in sin? And since we are lost, we are lost!" Thus it is better to rely on the authorities who permit this as a matter of halacha without any further strictures and bring them closer to God, Torah and mitzvot.

The concern Rabbi Ovadia Yosef feels is one worth thinking about. There might well be situations of outreach where one of the first steps toward bringing people back into the fold occurs when the couple comes to get married. Yet, nothing drives people away from Judaism and Torah faster than having their choice of a spouse rejected by their faith. Thus, in an Orthodox society which views outreach as a central part of its mission and recognizes the need to bring people to regular observance of Torah and mitzvot, Rabbi Ovadia Yosef's point seems to this writer to be correct and a ground to be lenient.[38]

---

38. The compulsory nature of rabbinic authority in Israel, given the exclusive jurisdiction of the rabbinical courts in Israel governing matters of marriage, also increases one's sense that matters of doubt should be resolved leniently by the rabbinical courts of Israel, as it seems halachically problematic to compel anyone to follow one normative school of thought over another normative school of thought within the halachic tradition. Each has the right to seek out their own rabbinic guidance on matters in dispute, at least in the absence of a communal norm – which is certainly lacking in this case.

About the author

Michael J. Broyde is a Professor of Law at Emory University School of Law and a Senior Fellow at Emory University's Center for the Study of Law and Religion. He served for many years as the *Yoshev Rosh* (chair) and a *dayan* (judge) in the SouthEast Rabbinical Court for Conversion, which was part of the GPS Conversion network. He also served as a *dayan* in the Beth Din of America and as its director. He was the Founding Rabbi of the Young Israel in Atlanta as well, where he served for many years as the rabbi. A summer grant from Emory University School of Law supported the writing of this work, as did a grant from the Tam Institute of Jewish Studies at Emory University.

Acknowledgments

Thank you to Rabbi Dr. Shlomo Pill and Dr. Akiva Berger, both of whom worked on this matter. I would like to thank Rabbi Dr. Gidon Rothstein, who thoughtfully commented on an early draft of this work, Rabbi Ari Enkin, who edited a draft, and Rabbi Dr. Elisha Ancselovits, who closely edited a late version. My thanks to the many people who read and edited earlier versions of this work, particularly to Victoria Razin and Amy Katz, whose editorial help was much appreciated. I am grateful to Rabbi Dr. Michael Berger, Rabbi Yossi New, and Rabbi Dr. Don Seeman, who sat with me on many conversion matters. I am grateful beyond words to the many converts I have been honored to work with. I truly learned more than I could express, and this work is dedicated to them. All errors remain the author's.

A Short Note on the Intellectual History of this Work

For many years, both as a synagogue rabbi and as the head of a rabbinical court for conversion, I was very much involved in conversion. Since that time, I have received many different questions from converts and children of converts about matters of Jewish law related to their status as a convert. I was surprised that no one had addressed these questions systematically and I had found little theoretical discussion. So I undertook to do that research and write such a work.

I committed to examine this literature at some length over the course of many years. Besides the many questions that I was asked, I undertook as complete a review of the responsa literature as I could find, collecting as many different cases as I encountered, vastly aided by the Bar Ilan Responsa Project and the Otzar Haposkim database. I also started to keep track of many different discussions in the classical halachic literature as I encountered them, each in its own place. I started to look closely at the many different works on conversion that have appeared in the last century in order to collect the many different piecemeal discussions in each of them about post-conversion issues. Most importantly, I am indebted to the many Torah scholars who graciously spoke with me about these many different matters. I feel blessed by the Almighty to be able to gain insight from these many conversations. If I have any success in this issue, it is as a dwarf on the shoulders of giants. However, as a matter of policy, I have on the whole cited in this work the views that are published.

Since this work is a collection of topics discussed in many different places related to converts, it is certain that I have left topics out that ought to be included in this work, and I have perhaps accidentally introduced errors as well, as I collected topics. The reader is encouraged to please contact me at mbroyde@emory.edu to share either topics I should have addressed or errors that I made.

Index

Subject Index

Source and Author Index

Shulchan Aruch Index